Touring Scotland

A guide to help you plan the trip of a lifetime

by
Paul Bissett

For Tracey,
my constant companion.

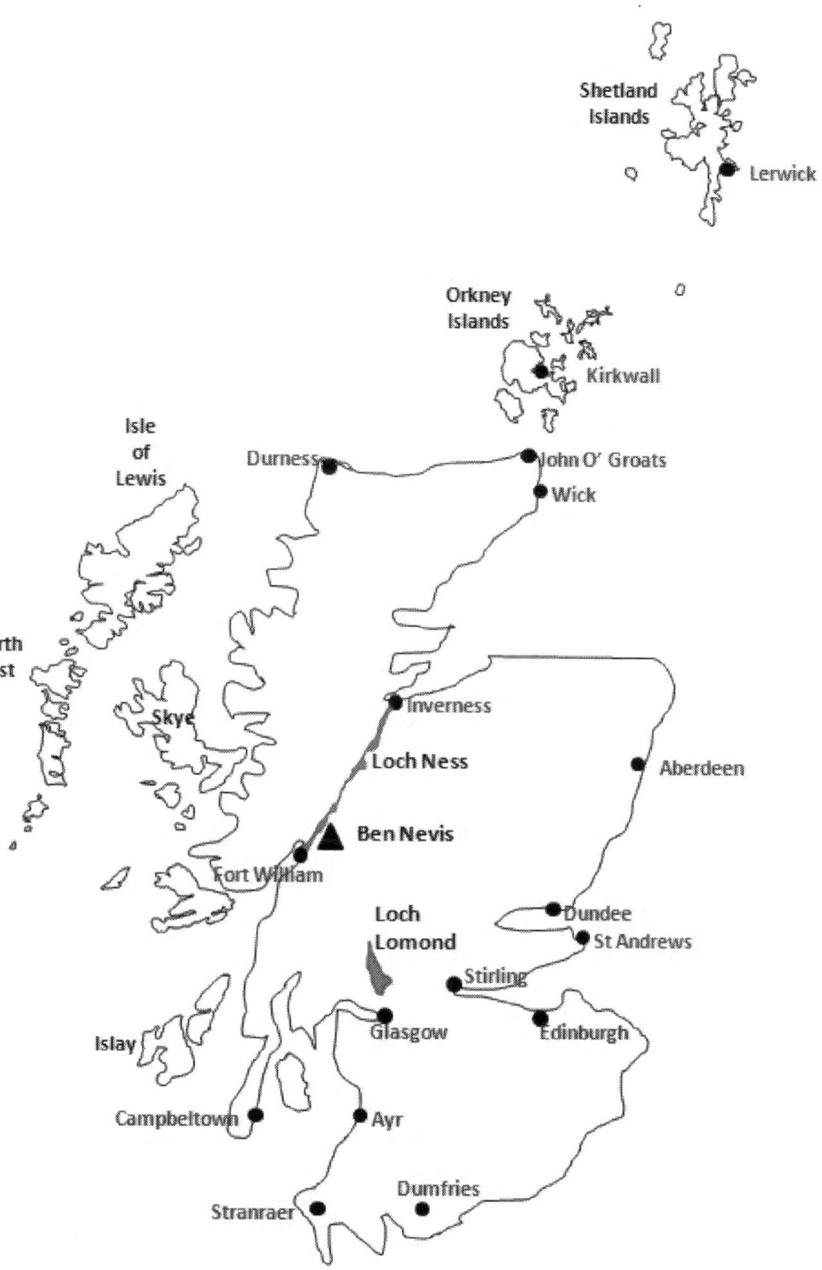

Map of Scotland

Table of Contents

	Aberdeen	Campbeltown	Edinburgh	Fort William	Glasgow	Inverness	Perth	Skye
Campbeltown	247							
Edinburgh	127	184						
Fort William	154	128	133					
Glasgow	145	140	47	108				
Inverness	104	194	156	66	168			
Perth	86	160	43	103	59	112		
Skye	206	209	227	99	209	106	183	
Stranraer	231	219	132	183	86	254	148	288

Mileage Chart

Chapter 1

Plan Your Trip

Having traveled to over forty countries and lived in seven, I have learned a thing or two about traveling, mainly through making mistakes, for instance;

We caught a ferry to France, but didn't bother changing money prior to boarding. Again, we couldhave changed our money on the ferry but didn't. Wethought (wrongly)we could change our pounds to francs when we got to France. When we arrived, my friends and I spent the day trying to get our money changed, with no luck, we spent the last few hours of our day trip in a bar at the ferry terminal that would accept British pounds. Lesson learned -- always change enough money to last a few days prior to leaving (not as important in this day of credit cards, but better safe than sorry).

You can change your money at the airport when you get there, after checking your bags and going through security (if the money exchange is open) or we have recently found it's fairly easy to find ATM's to take out local currencies from your local bank. It is still possible to order foreign currency from your bank before you leave (for a small fee, of course). It's also a very good idea to let your bank and credit card companies know the dates and destinations of your travel, so you don't have declined payments.

On another trip, my wife and I decided to tour around Europe and not book any accommodation in advance. Our plan (if you can call it that) was that if we liked a place, we would stay an extra day, if not we would move on. We flew into Frankfurt (when the Book Fair was on) and struggled to get a hotel. Where we stayed was less than ideal (to say the least). Next day we drove down to Munich for Octoberfest, knowing Munich would be booked out, we stopped in Augsburg about 50 miles north and tried to get a room. They told us the whole town was sold out for Octoberfest and the European Rodeo Finals (honest). We found a room at a farmhouse after hours of looking. After Octoberfest, we drove down South and tried to get a room in Oberammergau -- guess what? Their world renowned "Passion Play," which they put on once every ten years, was on that weekend; no hotels to be had.

A few days later we arrived in Paris at the same time as the European Auto Show was on – again, hotels booked out. It was the same when we got to Amsterdam. That trip makes for a funny story, over a few drinks, but was actually very stressful. So, book your rooms in advance; for some areas with limited accommodation, book as much as a year in advance, but also call up and confirm your booking with six months to go and again with three months to go.

We had a hotel in Scotland that changed ownership and lost our booking, fortunately we caught it at the six-month point.

On a different trip to Paris, apart from the obvious sites, we also wanted to see Rodin's Garden. Although we kept an eye open for it as we visited everything else, we never saw it. Each time we left the hotel we turned right, when the taxi picked us up to take us to the airport, it went left. Guess what was just around the corner; yes, it was Rodin's Garden.

It was at that point I decided to plan all future trips like they were a military campaign.When going on vacation, be it to a foreign country or a road trip, we discuss what we want to see and book our hotels based on that. I then research as much as possible, as to what there is to see and do in that area, also where to eat. This can mean that there are more things to see than time to see them. So, while there, we decide what we are going to see and what we're going to skip, based on how tired we are or what we have seen already. At least this way the choice is ours and we didn't miss something, that was just around the corner.

Something to consider when going to Scotland (well, the entirety of the UK) is driving.They drive on the left side of the road and their road signs and markings are usually different. If you drive an automatic at home, then be sure to book one in Scotland. I got a manual drive car in London and stalled it five times in the parking area before going back into the rental office and getting an automatic. If you are going rural in Scotland, the roads can be very narrow.So be aware that the bigger the car you get, the less room there is for other cars/trucks to get past you (and you them) on those narrow roads and it can be scary. We base the car size on the amount of luggage we have.

Do you even need a car? If you are staying in a city or large town there are buses/trams/taxis/trains to be had. We like to go all over Scotland, so usually do rent a car, but when we get back to Edinburgh (that's where we usually fly in and out from), we return the car to the rental office and take our luggage into town either by taxi or tram for the last few days of our vacation, as we don't need a car in Edinburgh and the traffic (and parking)can be really bad.
You can also stay in a town close by that has direct bus and train links, such as Linlithgow or Stirling.

Planning

You know you want to go to Scotland, but when exactly, and what do you want to see/do?Ideally, you will be thinking at least a year ahead. Can you book it in less time? Of course, you can, but if you are going into more rural areas, such as the Highlands, there are fewer accommodation options and they book out fast.
First, do a little research and make a list of what you want to see and do. This should also help you work out when you want to go, if for instance you want to go for Hogmanay (New Year) in Edinburgh, you will have to go in late December. If you wish to Visit the Edinburgh Festival, you go in August.
If you have no such date/time restraints, think about:

- The weather (historically, April and September have the least rain).

- Whatever time of year take a coat, it will likely rain at some point.

- Think about attractions being open (some close during the winter).

- Think about midges (See Additional Information in Chapter 13).

OK, you have your list and your dates.What I do now is look on Google maps to see where my priorities are geographically. This allows me to pick a start and finish point and overnight stays in between.
I now have a rough guide to my trip, but I don't book anything yet.
I continue working on Google maps and type in (for example)hotels in Fort William. This shows all the hotels and their prices. I can now pick a hotel location that works for us, usually based on walking distance to bars/restaurants, unless it is a destination hotel with everything we could need on premises.
I don't base the hotel selection on how close it is to something we want to visit (within reason), as we have the car, if that's how we're getting around(this is our preferred option as it is more flexible than public transport).
I now take the hotel information and research it online, Hotels.com, Kayak, Trip Advisor, Expedia etc., I find the best deal and make a note of it.We have found, through frustrating experience, that booking through one of these sites CAN greatly reduce any flexibility that might be needed. I prefer to book flights and hotels through their own websites as much as possible. You might need to get home sooner than expected or might even want to extend your trip – some of these travel websites are a

nightmare to get ahold of and/or won't let you change your itinerary.
Now it's time to work out how long it will take to get to our hotel via the things we want to see and do; how long it takes by car to our first stop.
I then allocate an approximate amount of time at our first stop, depending on what it is, then work out how long to our next stop and so forth.
This gives me a rough idea of how long a day it will be, and we can adjust as necessary. This may appear to be overkill, but it really does help to know what time you should set off and what time you can expect to arrive at your destination.

Here is an example day from our last trip;

Sat - Sep 29th (8.5 hours)

- Set off at 8:30am - 1.5 hour to Glamis Castle (opens at 10am - allow 2 hours to tour castle)

- 1 hour to the old course at St. Andrews for lunch (allow 1hour)

- 1.5 hours' drive to Dunnotter Castle (allow 1 hour to tour castle)

- 45 minutes to our hotel, McLeod Lodge (dinner booked)

Does it always work out the way I planned?
Not always.For instance, we ended up having a light lunch in the kitchen cafe at Glamis Castle and didn't go to St. Andrews for lunch. We also stopped in

Stonehaven after Dunnotter Castle, before carrying on to our hotel, but we made those informed choices because we knew our time constraints and what there was to see enroute.
What type of clothes should you take? Well, that will mainly be down to the time of year you choose to go. Choose layers so you can add or take off clothes as needed. No matter what time of year we go, we always take a rainproof coat or jacket. One trip, my wife, Tracey, forgot (wink-wink) a raincoat, so we stopped by a thrift store and she found one she liked for very little money. Comfortable shoes/boots are always a good idea. There are a lot of castles and other outdoor sites that need good footwear. I always take a baseball cap as it can keep the sun and rain out of your eyes. Other than that, just clothes that you are comfortable in, and something a bit dressier if you are planning a night out or a nice dinner.
The thing to remember is, you will have your suitcases with you in the car most of the time. You can almost always access extra clothing (if you have it with you). Also, if you need to, you can always buy something there.

Something to consider

Should you buy a pass or membership that gets you discounts to castles, stately homes or a city pass?We did a few years ago, but were disappointed to find that many of the sites we visited were not members, so had to pay anyway.
My suggestion is, if you are considering it, make a list of which sites you want to visit and check that against

what the pass gets you into, if it's a match, go ahead it will save you money.
But be aware that some passes are time sensitive, such as the "Edinburgh City Pass." This pass will save you 25% on normal entrance fees, but is only good for 48 hours, so you had better be committed to getting around the attractions.

Eating out

From food trucks to Michelin Starred restaurants, you are spoiled for choice. Scotland has great locally sourced food, from its abundant seafood, game, Black Angus (Aberdeen Angus) beef, andlamb, to its fruits and berries. You can pair great meals with any number of whiskies or gins, fine local ales and imported wines (we don't have the weather for grapes).
Suffice it to say that we have eaten in fish-n-chip shops, bars, pubs, diners, and Michelin Starred restaurants. We haven't had a bad meal and have had some memorable ones.
Be brave and try some of the local dishes like haggis (Scotland is the only place where it is made properly due to other countries' restrictions on the contents).On our last trip we both had haggis on the first four days. Dishes such asCullen Skink (fish soup), tattie scones, (potato scones), cranachan(dessert), scotch pies, black pudding, red pudding, white pudding (savories, not "pudding" in any American sense), stovies (variation on corned beef hash) and Arbroath Smokies (smoked fish) should be given a try.

Hotels

I was born and raised in Scotland and most of my family still live there. On several occasions we have stayed with family and used their house (or holiday home) as a base for our trips. Where we have stayed in a hotel, I have mentioned it. We have been happy with all our accommodations in Scotland, comparing what we paid for it, against the quality of the room and the service we received.
Please remember that hotel ownership may change, so your stay may differ from ours. Just because we liked it, does not guarantee that you will.
The one thing I will not do, is book a room in a hotel that does not have a website. Does that guarantee everything will be perfect? No, it doesn't, but I like to get an idea of what the hotel looks like and what is on offer there. So far, it has worked out for us.

Populations

I have given populations (approx.) of towns as a rough guide to what you may expect as far as amenities that may be available by the size of the population.

Maps

The map at the start of each chapter shows the area that is covered in that chapter. This is a general guide and I recommend that you get a proper map to plan your trip with and take it with you. Being from Scotland, I was taking my American wife around and she asked for a map so she could get a better perspective of where things were. We bought a Collins Road Map Scotland.

GPS

I'm now going to state the obvious, if you are using a GPS, be aware that it will take you the most direct route. For instance, if you are starting the day in Ullapool and intend to finish the day at Wick, it will take you by the shortest route across country and you will miss about half of the NC500.
Look at the map and use your GPS for waypoints such as Durness, then John O' Groats etc.

Compass Icon

You will see the above icon throughout the book. This is meant to give a general direction of where you will be heading. Obviously, (especially on the west coast) with all the twists and turns around lochs it can only be general.

I have listed points of interest by the direction they are from a set point in a city/town, so that if you are heading north to see one thing, you will know what is also in that direction. I have further divided each area down by giving new anchor points as you travel, for instance if you travel north to Stirling from Glasgow, I then give directions from Stirling Castle, before heading back north to Loch Lomondfrom Glasgow. This way I have tried to break each area down into smaller chunks. Hopefully, this will save you time by you not having to go back over the same ground the next day. Points are listed in North, South, East, and West order.

Chapter 2

Central Scotland

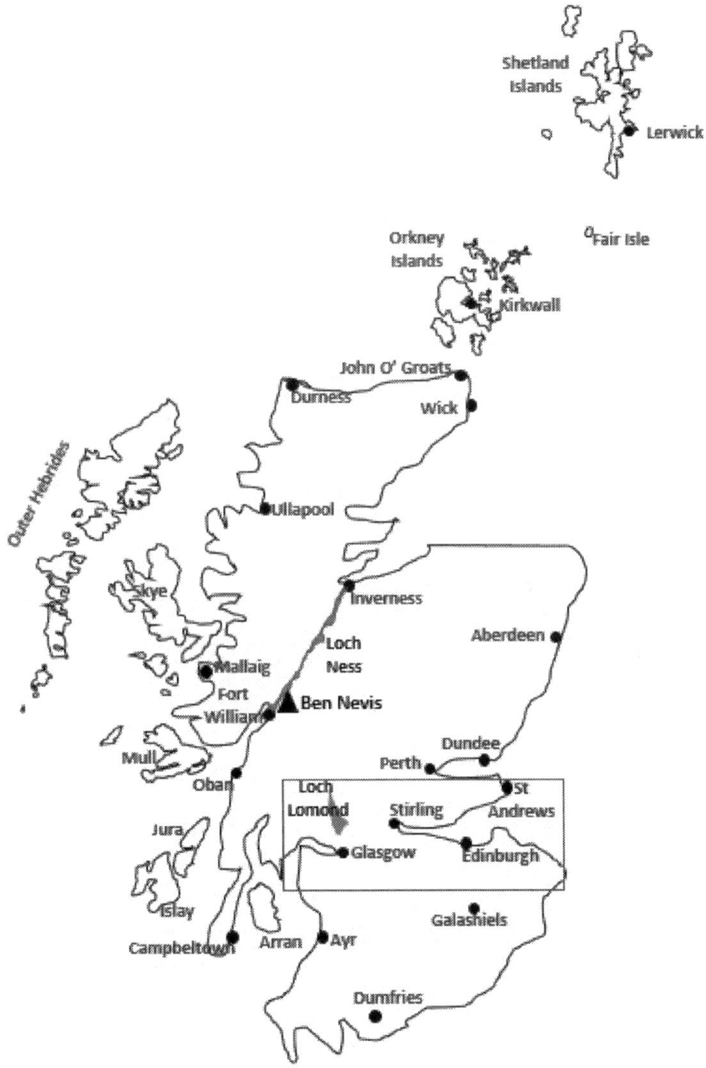

Edinburgh (Pop. 500,000)

(Pronounced Edin – Burra)

The capital of Scotland is a very walkable city and also has great public transport, should you need it. Edinburgh is roughly divided into two areas, the "Old Town" and the "New Town" (it's actually over 200-years-old) with Princes Street running between the two.
The "Old Town" is to the south (the area around the castle and the Royal Mile) and the "New Town" to the North. There is a wealth of things to do and see; in fact, so much to see and do that you could spend a full vacation in Edinburgh ... though you really should get out of the capitol and see the rest of Scotland.
If you are a movie fan, there have been many films shot in Edinburgh. Should you wish to see the locations of your favorite movies go to;
www.filmedinburgh.org/Filmed-Here
A great resource for movie fans.

Edinburgh International Airport (8 miles from the Scott Monument)

- With good transportation links into the city, and all the other facilities you'd expect from an international airport.
  www.edinburghairport.com

Hotels

There are hotels, B&Bs, and hostels available all over Edinburgh; to say that you're spoiled for choice would not be an exaggeration. If you are looking for something a bit more historical, then see;
Chapter 9 – Stay in a Castle or Stately home.
We stayed in the following hotels on our last few trips, and can recommend all of them;

Apex Grassmarket hotel

- Located in the historic Grassmarket area in the heart of Edinburgh, just a 2-minute walk from the Royal Mile, the 3 Star Grassmarket Hotel is a perfect base to explore the city!
  www.apexhotels.co.uk

The Angel's share hotel

- This hotel is a showcase of contemporary Scottish culture. With an impressive range of premium whisky, live music and a restaurant that showcases the finest modern cuisine made from fresh, locally sourced ingredients.
  https://angelssharehotel.com

The Balmoral hotel (Built in 1902)

- Sitting at the junction of Princes street and the bridge up to the Royal Mile. This luxury five-star hotel is an Edinburgh landmark. Their Whisky bar appropriately named "Scotch" has over 500 whiskies on offer.
  www.roccofortehotels.com

The Scotsman hotel(Built in 1905)

- Taking its name from the national newspaper that used to inhabit the building, this luxury hotel has stunning views across Edinburgh.
  https://scotsmanhotel.co.uk

Things to do and see - What's walk-able;

This is assuming that you are based in or around the City Center (within a mile of Princes Street Gardens). Obviously, what some people would consider walkable, others would not. My wife and I have walked to most of the places on this list. But just knowing that they are walkable means that, should you be thinking to take a taxi instead, you could save the fare.
There are many indoor places (museums, art galleries etc.) that I'd recommend you leave until towards the end of your trip.

That way if you get a rainy day, you can visit one or more of them, if you are very fortunate with the weather, they will be waiting for you to get to them.

Arthur's Seat (Free)

- The highest point in Holyrood park and an extinct volcano. Great views over the city, around 2 hours of walking. www.historicenvironment.scot/visit-a-place/places/holyrood-park

Calton Hill(Free)

- Historic monuments dating back to the Enlightenment (18th century) and great views. www.edinburghguide.com/parks/caltonhill

Camera Obscura & Rooftop Terrace.

- 360-degree panoramic views over Edinburgh. Five floors of fun things to do for all ages, whatever the weather. Scotland's oldest purpose-built attraction established in 1835. www.camera-obscura.co.uk
  The Royal Mile, Edinburgh.

City Art Center(normally free, depending on exhibits)

- Located in the heart of Edinburgh close to Waverley train station, the City Art Centre's aim is to champion historic and contemporary Scottish visual and applied arts. www.edinburghmuseums.org.uk/venue/city-art-centre
  2 Market Street, Edinburgh.

Dean Village(Free)

- Take a walk along the river of Leith through a medieval village. www.visitscotland.com/info/see-do/dean-village-p1419651

Edinburgh International Film Festival

- This two week-long festival is the oldest continuously running Film Festival in the world. Held annually in late-June. www.edfilmfest.org.uk

Edinburgh International Book Festival

- With over 100 free events held around the city over the last two weeks of August. www.edbookfest.co.uk

Edinburgh Fringe Festival

The Edinburgh Festival Fringe is the world's largest arts festival, held over the last three weeks of August and featuring more than 50,000 performances of 3,500 different shows at over 300 venues throughout the city.
www.eif.co.uk

Edinburgh International Festival

- The Festival's program features the finest performers and ensembles from the worlds of dance, opera, music and theatre. Held annually in the last three weeks of August.
  www.eif.co.uk

Edinburgh Whisky Festival

- Held annually in Early-June. Held in the Assembly rooms on George Street.
  https://thewhiskylounge.com

Edinburgh Whisky Stramash

- Held annually in Late-May. Set in the opulent and historic Surgeon's Hall on Nicholson Street.
  www.thewhiskystramash.com

The Royal Military Tattoo

- Held annually every August and performed by British, Commonwealth and international Military bands in Edinburgh Castle. www.edintattoo.co.uk

Scottish International Storytelling Festival

- Twelve-day celebration held at the end of October each year with storytelling, oral traditions. Bringing together Scottish and International storytellers and musicians. Various venues throughout Edinburgh. www.sisf.org.uk

Hogmanay Street Party, Edinburgh

- This is the big one, with hundreds of thousands of people gathered to welcome in the New Year. The party starts at 7:30pm on Hogmanay (New Year's Eve) and carries on into the wee hours of January 1st. Be entertained by international bands, DJs and street performers. At midnight a spectacular fireworks display illuminates the sky over Edinburgh Castle. www.edinburghshogmanay.com *Princes Street Gardens.*

Distilleries

- **Holyrood Distillery**
  The first single malt whisky distillery in the City Center in almost a century has newly opened. So, no Whisky yet, but it does have its own gin and a variety of tours (book online).
  www.holyrooddistillery.co.uk
  19 St Leonard's Lane, Edinburgh.

- **Summerhall Distillery**
  Home of Pickering's Gin. Tours available, book online.
  https://pickeringsgin.com
  1 Summerhall, Edinburgh.

- **The Edinburgh Gin Distillery**
  Tours (Book in advance online) and tastings, with two venues.
  www.edinburghgin.com/distilleries-and-tours
  1A Rutland Place, Edinburgh.
  4-6 Anderson Place, Edinburgh.

Edinburgh Castle

One of the oldest castles in Europe.

- Great views over the city
- Mons Meg (Medieval Canon)
- National War Museum
- Royal Military Tattoo (August each year)
- Scottish National War Memorial
- The Honors of Scotland (Crown Jewels)
- The Stone of Destiny
  www.edinburghcastle.scot
  Castlehill, Edinburgh.

Gin Cruises

- **Summerhall Drinks Lab** - 2 hour cruise (5 Gins) along the Union Canal.
  www.summerhalldrinkslab.co.uk/cruises.html

Greyfriars Bobby

- Edinburgh policeman, John Gray, acquired a stray black terrier he called "Bobby" to serve as a watch dogand theybecame inseparable until Gray died of tuberculosis. A funeral procession to the gravesite at Greyfriars Kirk yard was led by the dog.
  With interment complete, Bobby attempted to stay by his master's covered grave, but many times the caretaker sent him packing, but Bobby persisted, keeping watch over the grave. Local residents fed the dog and even built him a shelter. A tradition at nearby Edinburgh Castle is the firing of a cannon to signal the one o'clock hour, which also would find Bobby trotting out heading for a restaurant called 'Traill's Dining Rooms,' where the proprietor regularly gave Bobby his lunch and where Constable John Gray often had his lunch while making his rounds.
  When word of this spread around the country, crowds would collect at the gates of the Kirk yard to see this amazing event. Bobby was all business; he did not linger over his food. Finished, he raced off to the cemetery to continue his vigil. Nine years after the death of his master, Bobby was seized as a homeless dog without a collar or license.
  The Lord Provost of Edinburgh was so touched by his loyalty, that he personally paid the annual dog license while presenting the dog with a brass-plated collar inscribed: 'Greyfriars Bobby, from the Lord Provost, 1867, Licensed'.

This ritual lasted fourteen years until Bobby died and was buried inside Greyfriars Kirk yard, about 75 yards from John Gray's grave. The dog caught the attention of Baroness Burdett-Coutts fearing the animal would be forgotten in death, was instrumental in having a permanent memorial build in recognition of Bobby's loyalty.
Completed in 1872. It is mounted on a granite pylon at the sharp junction of George IV Bridge and Candlemaker Row in Edinburgh just opposite the entrance to Greyfriars Kirk.
With thanks to "**Find a Grave**" website.
www.findagrave.com/memorial/5637/greyfriars_bobby

Greyfriars Church

- Built on the site of a pre-Reformation Franciscan monastery, the iconic building offers much to see and appreciate, including the National Covenant (signed here in the Kirk yard in 1638).
  https://greyfriarskirk.com
  26A Candlemaker Row, Edinburgh.

High Teas(Afternoon Teas)

- **A Brief History of Afternoon Tea**
  Afternoon tea was purported to have started in the mid-1800s by the Duchess of Bedford. Around this time, kerosene lamps were introduced in wealthier homes, and eating a late dinner (around eight or nine PM) became fashionable. At the time, there were only two meals each day a mid-morning, brunch and the other was a late dinner.
  The story goes that the Duchess found herself with a "sinking feeling" (likely fatigue from hunger during the long wait between meals) and decided to have some friends over for assorted snacks and tea (a very fashionable drink at the time). The idea of afternoon tea soon spread across High Society (probably where the mistaken term "High Tea" comes from).

- **Afternoon tea**, also known as "Low Tea," is what most people think of when they hear "High Tea." It involves things like manners, lace and dainty foods. It is typically served in the mid-afternoon and it was traditionally served on low tables, hence its two names.

- **High Tea**was a working-class meal served on a high table at the end of the workday, shortly after five PM. Basically it was just another name for dinner.

Just a few of the many Teas available;

- **Colonnades at the Signet Library**
  Home of the Society of Writers to Her Majesty's Signet, a prestigious legal association – Open to the public.
  www.thesignetlibrary.co.uk/colonnades
  The Signet Library, Parliament Square, Edinburgh.

- **Gateway Restaurant at the Royal Botanical Gardens**.
  www.rbge.org.uk/media/5020/autumn-afternoon-tea-menu.pdf
  Arboretum Place, Edinburgh.

- **Georgian Tea Room at the Dome.**
  www.thedomeedinburgh.com/georgiantearoom
  14 George Street, Edinburgh.

- **The Palm Court at the Balmoral Hotel**
  www.roccofortehotels.com
  1 Princes Street.

- **The Tea Room in Crown Square at Edinburgh Castle.**
  www.edinburghcastle.scot/whats-on/afternoon-tea-experience
  Castlehill, Edinburgh.

- **Tower Restaurant at the National Museum of Scotland.**
  www.nms.ac.uk/national-museum-of-scotland/plan-your-visit/eating-at-the-museum
  National Museum of Scotland, Chambers Street, Edinburgh.

Holyrood House

- The official residence in Scotland of Her Majesty the Queen. Many historic figures such as Mary, Queen of Scots and Bonnie Prince Charlie spent time here. Open throughout the year.
  www.rct.uk/visit/palace-of-holyroodhouse
  Canongate, Edinburgh.

Johnny Walker Whisky Experience.

- Opening soon.
  www.diageo.com
  142-144 Princes Street, Edinburgh.

Magdalen Chapel (Free)

- The Chapel was built in 1544. The building was to be the new chapel for the Incorporation of Hammermen and was to include accommodation for a chaplain and also an almshouse for seven Bedesmen (poor men) 'who should continually pour forth prayers to Almighty God.' In particular they were to pray for the soul of Mary Queen of Scots.
  The Royal Arms of Scotland and the Arms of the Queen Regent, Mary of Guise, can be seen in the middle window in the south wall of the chapel. The stained glass in this window is the only pre-Reformation stained glass in Scotland which is still intact.
  www.scottishreformationsociety.org/the-magdalen-chapel
  41 Cowgate, Edinburgh.

Museum of Childhood

- The Museum of Childhood was the first museum in the world to be dedicated to the history of childhood and it attracts over 200,000 visitors a year. Amongst the displays you will find toys, games, clothes, books and dolls, dating from the 1800s to the present day.
  www.edinburghmuseums.org.uk/venue/museum-childhood
  42 High St, Edinburgh.

Museum of Edinburgh(Free)

- Explore Edinburgh's history.
  www.edinburghmuseums.org.uk/venue/museum-edinburgh
  142-146 Canongate, Royal Mile.

Museum on the Mound(Free)

- Located in the historic Bank of Scotland Head Office, this fascinating museum takes a fresh look at money – and much, much more. Art & design, technology, crime, trade and security – all feature in the story of money.
  https://museumonthemound.com
  The Mound, Edinburgh.

National Museum of Scotland (Free)

- Showcasing Scottish history and so much more.
  www.nms.ac.uk/national-museum-of-scotland
  Chambers Street, Edinburgh.

Old Calton Burial Ground(Free)

- This Graveyard sits just below Calton hill on the other side of the street and is home to a statue of former American president, Abraham Lincoln. He stands atop a memorial to the Scottish soldiers who fought for the Union in the American Civil War, this is the only American Civil War memorial outside of North America. The statue of Lincoln was the first statue of an American president to be built outside of the United States when it was erected in 1893.
  Waterloo Place, Edinburgh.

Princes Street Gardens(Free)

- Beautiful public park that sits below the castle and runs parallel with the shops on Princes street.
  www.edinburghoutdoors.org.uk
  Princes Street.

Royal Botanic Garden(established in 1670)

- Need to relax for a few hours? Then visit one of the world's leading botanic gardens and walk around 70 acres of beautiful landscape.
  www.rbge.org.uk
  Arboretum Place, Edinburgh.

Scott Monument

- Standing proudly in Princes Street Gardens, the Scott Monument is one of the most iconic Edinburgh landmarks, a must-visit for tourists and locals alike. Dedicated to Sir Walter Scott, it is one of the largest monuments to a writer anywhere in the world. The views from the top are amazing, well worth the effort to climb the 287 steps up the narrow spiral staircase.
  www.edinburghmuseums.org.uk/venue/scott-monument
  E. Princes Street Gardens, Edinburgh.

Surgeons' Hall Museums

- As one of the oldest Museums in Scotland, the collections grew from 1699 after 'natural and artificial curiosities' were publicly sought. Whilst the Museums were initially established as a medical teaching resource, they are now open to the public.
  https://museum.rcsed.ac.uk
  Surgeons Hall Museums, Nicolson Street, Edinburgh.

The Chocolatarium

- Working Chocolate Museum, take a tour and learn about everything chocolate. Make your own chocolate souvenir to take home (age 8 and up).
  www.chocolatarium.co.uk
  3-5 Cranston Street, Edinburgh.

The Grassmarket(Free)

- Just off the Royal Mile and in the shadow of the castle, along cobbled streets, sits the Grassmarket. With shops restaurants and historic pubs, which have witnessed many interesting times including; the terror of Burke and Hare, Public Executions, Deacon Brodie, Jacobite soldiers and the Highland Drover Cattle Markets.

The People's Story Museum

- This Museum gives a unique insight in to Edinburgh's working-class people from the 18th century to the late 20th century.
  www.edinburghmuseums.org.uk/venue/peoples-story-museum
  The Royal Mile, 163 Canongate, Edinburgh.

The Royal Mile(walking and looking Free)

- The street connecting the Castle at the top and Holyrood House at the bottom, there is a fee on some of the attractions.

    - Closes (Alleys off the main street),
    - Real Mary King's close (underground tour).
    - Museums
    - Pubs and Restaurants
    - Shops
    - St Giles Cathedral
    - The Scotch Whisky Experience
    - Underground tours

Writer's Museum(Free)

- The Writers' Museum celebrates the lives of three giants of Scottish Literature – Robert Burns, Robert Louis Stevenson and Walter Scott.
  www.edinburghmuseums.org.uk/venue/writers-museum
  Lawnmarket, Lady Stair's Close, Edinburgh.

Things to do and see What's <u>not</u> walk-able;

For your travels out of Edinburgh I have used the "Scott Monument" on Princes street (City Center) as my anchor point for distances to the various sites listed below as the "Scott Monument" is hard to miss for first time visitors to Edinburgh due to its size and its central location in Edinburgh.

North from Edinburgh City Center

The Royal Yacht Britannia(3 miles from the Scott Monument)

- Her Majesty Queen Elizabeth's former floating palace for over 40 years, Now Moored in Leith. There are many buses and there are always taxis. We walked there and caught a bus back. www.royalyachtbritannia.co.uk
  Ocean Drive, Leith, Edinburgh.

The National Museums Collection Center (3 miles North from the Scott Monument)

- Home to many of the objects and specimens that are not currently on display in our museums. Guided tours. www.nms.ac.uk/collectioncentre

Lauriston Castle (4 miles North & West from the Scott Monument)

- Picturesque stately home with Edwardian decor. www.edinburghmuseums.org.uk/venue/lauriston-castle
  2 Cramond Road South, Edinburgh.

North across the bridges into the Kingdom of Fife

Inverkeithing Highland Games (14 miles North from the Scott Monument)

- Held in Early-August each year. Tossing the Caber, Highland dancing, Athletics, and Pipe bands. http://inverkeithinghighlandgames.com/hg
  Ballast Bank, Inverkeithing.

Dunfermline(Pop. 50,000)

(17 miles West and North from the Scott Monument)

The town (and former capitol) was first recorded in the 11th century, with the marriage of King Malcolm the 3rd to his wife Margaret (later Saint Margaret), at the church in Dunfermline. There are good bus and rail links to Edinburgh. I will be using Dunfermline Abbey as a base for distances to sites/places in the area.

- Hotels, B&Bs, Food, Drink, Car Hire, Buses, Taxis, Shops, ATMs/Banks, Hospital, Museum, **Gas (petrol) & Charging Stations**.

Andrew Carnegie Birthplace Museum

- Andrew Carnegie (American Billionaire) was one of the great Scots of the 19th century. Entrepreneur, lecturer, philanthropist, Steel tycoon, stockbroker, writer. Quote "*Any man who dies rich, dies disgraced...*"
  www.carnegiebirthplace.com
  Moody Street.

Dunfermline Abbey

- Formerly a Benedictine Abbey founded by Queen Margaret in the 11th century. The foundations of the church that King Malcolm and his queen Margaret married in are under the present abbey, built by their son King David the 1st. King Robert the Bruce's body is buried here, but his heart is buried in Melrose Abbey.
https://dunfermlineabbey.com

Dunfermline Carnegie Library & Galleries(Free)

- Museum, gallery spaces, cafe, shop and reading rooms.
https://onfife.com

Pittencrief House

- Built in the 17th century and open to the public. The house and 76-acre park were given to the town by Andrew Carnegie the American Billionaire (Born in Dunfermline) in 1903.
www.thecastlesofscotland.co.uk

St Margaret's Cave (Free)

- Queen Margaret (Saint) came regularly to pray at this cave over 900 years ago.
  www.onfife.com
  Chalmers Street.

North from Dunfermline Abbey

Loch Leven Castle (12 miles North from Dunfermline Abbey)

- Built in the 1300s, Mary Queen of Scots was held captive here. The ferry over the loch to the island is included in the ticket price.
  www.historicenvironment.scot
  Pier Road, Kinross.

St Serf's Church and Dupplin Cross (23 miles North from Dunfermline Abbey)

- Built around the year 1200. The Dupplin Cross is also to be found here – a superb Pictish carving of the early 9th century.
  www.historicenvironment.scot
  Tron Square, Dunning.

Gleneagles Hotel (24 miles North from Dunfermline Abbey)

- Built in the 1924, thesis one of the world's great hotel estates, with 232 luxury rooms and 27 suites,3 full size world-class golf courses and a 9-hole course. There is Salmon fishing, Landrover off-road driving and tThe hotel is home to the British School of Falconry. With 10 top notch restaurants and Bars.
  https://gleneagles.com
  Auchterarder.

Blackford Highland Games (25 miles North from Dunfermline Abbey)

- Held Late-May each year. Tossing the Caber, Highland dancing, Athletics, and Pipe bands.
  http://blackfordhighlandgames.co.uk
  Blackford, Auchterarder.

East from Dunfermline Abbey

Aberdour Castle (8 miles East from Dunfermline Abbey)

- Possibly Scotland's oldest standing Castle, built in the 1100s.
  www.historicenvironment.scot
  Aberdour.

Burntisland Highland Games(11 miles East from Dunfermline Abbey)

- Held in Late-July each year. Tossing the Caber, Highland dancing, Athletics, and Pipe bands.
  https://burntislandhighlandgames.co.uk
  Burntisland Links, Kinghorn Road, Burntisland.

Thornton Highland Gathering(17 miles East from Dunfermline Abbey)

- Held in Early-July each year. Tossing the Caber, Highland dancing, Athletics, and Pipe bands.
  www.shga.co.uk
  Main Street, Thornton.

Markinch Highland Games (20 miles East from Dunfermline Abbey)

- Held in early-June each year. Tossing the Caber, Highland dancing, Athletics, and Pipe bands.
  www.shottshighlandgames.org.uk
  John Dixon Park, Markinch, Glenrothes.

Falkland Palace (23 miles East from Dunfermline Abbey)

- Built in the 16th century this is one of the finest examples of Renaissance architecture in Scotland.
  www.nts.org.uk
  East Port, Falkland, Cupar.

Lundin Standing Stones (24 miles East from Dunfermline Abbey)

- 3 standing stones dating to the Bronze Age and reaching about 17 feet high.
  www.britainexpress.com
  Lundin Links, Leven.

Hill of Tarvit Mansion (29 miles East from Dunfermline Abbey)

- Edwardian Mansion with its own golf course.
  www.nts.org.uk
  Cupar.

Ceres Highland Games(Free)
(30 miles East from Dunfermline Abbey)

- Held in Late-June each year. Tossing the Caber, Highland dancing, Athletics, and Pipe bands.
  www.ceresgames.co.uk
  St Andrews Road, Ceres, Cupar.

Cupar Highland Games(30 miles East from Dunfermline Abbey)

- Held in Mid-June each year. Tossing the Caber, Highland dancing, Athletics, and Pipe bands.
  http://cuparhighlandgames.org
  41 Carslogie Road, Cupar.

Fife Whisky Festival(31 miles East from Dunfermline Abbey)

- Held in Early-March each year. This is a 3-day Festival for the appreciation of Whisky. https://fifewhiskyfestival.com
St Catherine Street, Cupar.

The East Neuk of Fife

(31 miles East from Dunfermline Abbey)

The 'East Neuk' or eastern corner of the 'Kingdom of Fife' is one of Scotland's hidden gems. Consisting of a number of small former fishing villages, stretching from the villages of Elie & Earlsferry to Crail and Kingsbarns.
Lots of photo opportunities and good food, with some of the best Fish and Chips to be had in the UK.

St Andrews(Pop. 17,000)

(37 miles East from Dunfermline Abbey)

St Andrews university was founded in 1410, making it the oldest in Scotland. In medieval times St Andrews was the religious capital of Scotland, and its cathedral was the most important in the country.
As you are no doubt aware St Andrews is also the "home of golf," with the Royal and Ancient being one of the oldest Golf Clubs in the world. There are several golf courses or "links", including the renowned Old Course which can be played, but you had better book in advance. A number of local hotels can get you tee times as a package when you book a stay with them.
The Nearest Airport is Dundee Airport (12 miles away).
The nearest train station is at Leuchars (6 miles away)
There are good bus services available.

- Hotels, B&Bs, Food, Drink, Car Hire, Buses, Taxis, Shops, ATMs/Banks, Hospital, Museum,**Gas (petrol) & Charging Stations**.

British Golf Museum

- With the largest collection of golfing memorabilia in Europe.
  www.britishgolfmuseum.co.uk
  St Andrews.

Eden Mill Distillery

- Pronunciation: Eden-mill.
- Name Origin: Named after the mill that was there prior to the distillery.
- Established: 2012.
- Location: Main Street, Guardbridge, St Andrews.
- Region: Lowland.
- Visitor Center/Tours: Go to website for information.
- Website:www.edenmill.com

St Andrews Brewing Company

- Brewery and restaurant.
  www.standrewsbrewingcompany.com
  St Andrews.

St Andrews Castle

- Now a ruin, St Andrews Castle was a bishop's palace, a fortress and a state prison during its 450-year history.
  www.historicenvironment.scot
  St Andrews.

St Andrews Cathedral

- Now a ruin, Scotland's largest and most magnificent medieval church is still well worth a visit.
  www.historicenvironment.scot
  St Andrews.

St Andrews Highland Games

- Held in Late-July each year. Tossing the Caber, Highland dancing, Athletics, and Pipe bands.
  www.standrewshighlandgames.co.uk
  Station Park, St Andrews.

St Andrews Museum (Free)

- Housed in a Victorian mansion in the grounds of Kilnburn Park. Showing the history of St Andrews from the 12th century to the present day.
  www.onfife.com
  St Andrews.

St Andrews University

- St Andrews university was founded in 1410, making it the oldest in Scotland and the 3rd oldest in the English-speaking world.
  www.st-andrews.ac.uk
  St Andrews.

St Andrews University - Bell Pettigrew Museum

- The Museums' collections are of national and international interest and importance and consist of around 115,000 artefacts and specimens.
  www.st-andrews.ac.uk/museums
  St Andrews.

St Andrews University -St Salvator's Chapel

- Founded in 1450 by Bishop James Kennedy.
  www.st-andrews.ac.uk/about/history/st-salvators
  St Andrews.

St Andrews University - Wardlaw Museum

- The Museums' collections are of national and international interest and importance and consist of around 115,000 artefacts and specimens.
  www.st-andrews.ac.uk/museums
  St Andrews.

Kingsbarns Distillery (8 miles South from St Andrews)

- Pronunciation: Kings-barns.
- Name Origin: Kingsbarns farm.
- Established: 2014.
- Location: Kingsbarns, St Andrews.
- Region: Lowland.
- Visitor Center/Tours: Go to website for information.
- Website:www.kingsbarnsdistillery.com

Fernie Castle Hotel(15 miles West from St Andrews)

- First established in 1353, the present castle dates back almost 500 years.
  http://ferniecastle.co.uk
  Cupar.

Myers Castle Hotel(19 miles West from St Andrews)

- Built in 1530 and nestled in the Kingdom of Fife.
  www.myrescastle.co.uk
  Cupar.

Lindores Abbey Distillery(20 miles West from St Andrews)

- Pronunciation: Lin-Doors Abbey.
- Name Origin: Built at the site of Lindores Abbey.
- Established: 2017.
- Location: Abbey Road, Newburgh, Cupar.
- Region: Lowland.
- Visitor Center/Tours: Go to website for information.
- Website: https

West from Dunfermline Abbey

Culross Village(Pronounced Coo-Ross)

(9 miles West from Dunfermline Abbey)

Pituresque village with 16th and 17th century houses, used for scenes in Outlander.

Culross Abbey

- Ruined Abbey built in the 1200s.
  www.historicenvironment.scot

Culross Palace

- Not actually a palace, but a house built in the late 16th century.
  www.nts.org.uk

Clachmannan Tower (13 miles West from Dunfermline Abbey)

- 1300s tower house. www.historicenvironment.scot

Dollar Glen and Castle Campbell (14 miles West and North from Dunfermline Abbey)

- 15th century Castle Campbell is one of Scotland's best-preserved tower houses. Terraced gardens and enjoy spectacular views down Dollar glen. www.historicenvironment.scot

South from Edinburgh City Center

Craigmillar Castle (4 miles from the Scott Monument)

- Mary Queen of Scots famously used the castle as a safe haven in 1566.
  www.historicenvironment.scot

Rosslyn Chapel(8 miles South from the Scott Monument)

- Rosslyn Chapel was founded in 1446 as a place of worship and services continue to be held here weekly. The Chapel has become a major tourist destination since the book and more specifically the movie "The Da Vinci Code" by Dan Brown came out.
  www.rosslynchapel.com
  Chapel Loan, Roslin.

Chrichton Castle(15 miles South from the Scott Monument)

- Built in the late 1300s for the Crichton family, later as a residence for the Earls of Bothwell.
www.historicenvironment.scot
Crichton, Pathhead.

Glenkinchie Distillery(16 miles South/East from the Scott Monument)

There is a regular shuttle bus service departing Edinburgh City Center three times a day (twice on a Sunday).

- Pronunciation: Glen-Kin-Chee.
- Name Origin: Gaelic - "Valley of 'de Quincey,' the family that owned the land.
- Established:1837.
- Location: Pencaitland, Tranent, near Edinburgh.
- Region: Lowland.
- Visitor Center/Tours: Go to website for information.
- Website:www.malts.com/en-row/distilleries/glenkinchie

Peebles Highland Games (23 miles South from the Scott Monument)

- Held in Early-September each year. Tossing the Caber, Highland dancing, Athletics, and Pipe bands.
  www.peebleshighlandgames.com
  Hay Lodge Park, Old Town, Peebles.

Thirlestane Castle(28 miles South from the Scott Monument)

- Built originally as a defensive fort in the 13th century, it was re-built in the 16th century as a home.
  www.thirlestanecastle.co.uk
  Lauder.

East from Edinburgh City Center

Newhailes House and Estate(6 miles East from the Scott Monument)

- 17th-century Palladian villa.
  www.nts.org.uk/visit/places/newhailes
  Newhailes, Musselburgh.

Fa'side Castle Hotel(10 miles East from the Scott Monument)

- B&B accommodation situated at the top of the 14th century tower.
  www.faside-estate.com
  Tranent.

Chesters Hill Fort (21 miles East from the Scott Monument)

- One of Scotland's best-preserved Iron Age hillforts, with impressive ramparts and ditches.
  www.historicenvironment.scot
  East Lothian, North Berwick.

Dirleton Castle and Gardens (22 miles East from the Scott Monument)

- With some of the oldest castle architecture surviving in Scotland, the de Vaux towers, built around 1240.
  www.historicenvironment.scot
  Dirleton, North Berwick.

Flag Heritage Center(Free)
(22 miles East from the Scott Monument)

- According to tradition "The Saltire (St Andrews cross) Flag of Scotland originated at the battle of Athelstaneford in 832 AD. This may be a small museum, but it's the place to learn all about the Saltire.
  https://scottishflagtrust.com/the-flag-heritage-centre
  Athelstaneford, North Berwick.

Hailes Castle(23 miles East from the Scott Monument)

- Dating from the early 1200s, making it one of Scotland's oldest castles.
  www.nms.ac.uk/flight
  Haddington.

National Museum of Flight(23 miles East from the Scott Monument)

- East Fortune Airfield is the UK's best-preserved Second World War airfield. Many historic aircraft including Concorde.
  www.nms.ac.uk/flight
  East Fortune Airfield, North Berwick.

North Berwick Highland Games(28 miles East from the Scott Monument)

- Held in Early-August each year. Tossing the Caber, Highland dancing, Athletics, and Pipe bands.
  www.northberwickhighlandgames.org
  Recreation Park, Dunbar Road, North Berwick.

Dunbar Town House Museum &Gallery
(Free)
(30 miles East from the Scott Monument)

- The Town House features town life since the 16th century.
  www.eastlothian.gov.uk
  Dunbar.

Tantallon Castle(31 miles East from the Scott Monument)

- Medieval castle and home to the Red Douglas dynasty. Great viewpoint for seeing Bass Rock.
  www.historicenvironment.scot
  North Berwick.

St Abbs village(48 miles East from the Scott Monument)

- Small village used as "New Asgard" in the Marvel Movie "Avengers End Game."
  www.filmedinburgh.org/Filmed-Here/Avengers-Endgame
  St Abbs.

West from Edinburgh City Center

Edinburgh Zoo(4 miles West from the Scott Monument)

- Covering 82-acres on the south side of Corstorphine Hill and offering extensive views of the city. The zoo is involved in many scientific pursuits, such as Captive Breeding of endangered animals, research into Animal behavior, and is also active in many Conservation programs around the world.
  www.edinburghzoo.org.uk
  134 Corstorphine Road, Edinburgh.

Royal Highland Show (8 miles West of the Scott Monument, Edinburgh)

- Scotland's largest agricultural show held at Ingliston show grounds, attracting over 1,000 exhibitors, 4,500 head of livestock, and up to 200,000 visitors each year.
  www.royalhighlandshow.org

South Queensferry (Pop. 9,000)

(9 miles West from the Scott Monument)

The town takes its name from being on the south side of the ferry route (established by Queen Margaret almost 1,000 years ago) across the river Forth. Good rail and bus links to Edinburgh.

- Hotels, B&Bs, Food, Drink, Car Hire, Buses, Taxis, Shops, ATMs/Banks, **Gas (petrol) & Charging Stations**.

Bridges (Free to view, walk& Cycle)

The town of South Queensferry was named for a ferry but is now best known for the 3 bridges that span the Forth here. Each bridge being built in a different century and all still in use.

- The large red cantilevered bridge is for trains and was built in the 19th century (1890) and is still considered the strongest bridge in the world.
- The Suspension bridge (in the middle) was built in the 20th century (1964) and is comparable in size to San Francisco's Golden Gate Bridge.
- The Queensferry crossing bridge was built in the 21st century, the longest three-tower, cable-stayed bridge in the world. www.theforthbridges.org

Edinburgh Boat Charters

- Various sailing tours.
  www.edinburghboatcharters.com
  South Queensferry.

Hawes Inn

- Historic Inn, tucked under the Rail Bridge and mentioned in Robert Louis Stevenson's book "Kidnapped." It is believed that while staying at the Hawes inn he came up with the idea for his novel and even wrote some of the novel there.
  No Website.
  7 Newhalls Road, South Queensferry.

Maid of the Forth

- Boat tours under the bridges and tours of Incholm island.
  www.maidoftheforth.co.uk
  South Queensferry.

Dalmeny House

- This Tudor Gothic mansion was completed in 1817 and is home to the Earl and Countess of Rosebery.
  https://roseberyestates.co.uk/dalmeny-house
  South Queensferry.

Hopetoun House(3 miles West from South Queensferry)

- One of Scotland's finest stately homes, situated on the Firth of Forth (River)
https://hopetoun.co.uk
South Queensferry.

Binns House(17 miles West from the Scott Monument)

- Built in 1612 by Thomas Dalyell and set in landscaped parkland overlooking Blackness castle and the River Forth.
www.nts.org.uk/visit/places/house-of-binns
Binns View, Linlithgow.

Blackness Castle(17 miles West from the Scott Monument)

- One of Scotland's most impressive strongholds, Blackness Castle was built in the 15th century by one of Scotland's most powerful families, the Crichtons. Blackness Castle has been a royal castle, prison, and armaments depot. It has been used for film and TV locations for Hamlet, Mary Queen of Scots, Outlander and many other productions.
Blackness Castle is often referred to as 'the ship that never sailed' due to its great stone ship appearance.

From the castle you can enjoy breathtaking views of the Firth of Forth and Fife. (My friends and I used to play in the castle, when I was a child)
www.visitscotland.com
Blackness, near Linlithgow.

Bo'ness (Pop. 15,000)

(Pronounced Bow – Ness)
(18 miles west from the Scott Monument)

Its full name is *Borrowstounness*, ("the headland near Beornweard's farmstead").

- Hotels, B&Bs, Food, Drink, Car Hire, Buses, Taxis, Shops, ATMs/Banks, **Gas (petrol) & Charging Stations**.

Bo'ness and Kinneil Railway

- Ride a steam train and visit Scotland's largest Railway Museum.
  www.bkrailway.co.uk

Hippodrome Movie House

- Scotland's oldest (1911) purpose-built movie theater, totally refurbished and still showing films.
  www.hippodromecinema.co.uk

Kinneil House and Estate(Free)

- Dating back to the 16th century, with a museum displaying history back to the Roman occupation. Open 6 days a week, not Tuesdays.
  https://kinneil.org

Linlithgow (Pop. 13,000)

(Pronounced Lin – Lith - Go)
(19 miles west from the Scott Monument)

I went to High School here. Linlithgow is a good option to staying in Edinburgh, there are good bus and rail links to Edinburgh and Glasgow.

- Hotels, B&Bs, Food, Drink, Car Hire, Buses, Taxis, Shops, ATMs/Banks, Museum, **Gas (petrol) & Charging Stations**.

Linlithgow Palace

- The Palace was the birthplace of Mary Queen of Scots, and although now a ruin, it's an impressive ruin set in beautiful grounds alongside Linlithgow Loch.
  www.historicenvironment.scot/visit-a-place/places/linlithgow-palace
  Kirkgate, Linlithgow.

St Michaels Church

- In 1138 King David I, gifted the church to the Cathedral of St Andrews. Mary Queen of Scots was baptized here. My high School held its Easter and Christmas services here.
  www.stmichaelsparish.org.uk
  Kirkgate, Linlithgow.

Scottish Korean War Memorial(3 miles South from Linlithgow)

- The Memorial is an arboretum of 1,114 native Scottish trees, one for every man who died, and a shrine surrounded by two mounds in the shape of the Ying and Yang on the Korean flag. The shrine is built in the traditional style of a Korean shrine and contains name boards listing all the 1,114 men who died.
  www.historicenvironment.scot
  Bathgate.

Torphichen Preceptory(4 miles South from Linlithgow)

- Founded by King David I in the 1100s. It was the Scottish base of operations for the Knights Hospitaller.
  www.historicenvironment.scot
  Bowyett, Torphichen, Bathgate.

Glasgow(Pop. 600,000)

(Pronounced Glass – Go)

(473 miles West from Edinburgh)

Scotland's largest city and unlike Edinburgh not that walk-able, but it does have great public transport including an underground train system.
Glasgow is well served with transport links, including 2 international airports two main-line train stations (Queen Street and Central), an underground train system, National and local bus services.

Glasgow International Airport(9 miles West from George Square)

- With good transportation links into the city, and all the other facilities you'd expect from an international airport.
  www.glasgowairport.com

Prestwick International Airport(32 miles South West from George Square)

- With good transportation links into the city, including its own rail link and all the other facilities you'd expect from an international airport.
  www.glasgowprestwick.com

Hotels

There are Hotels, B&Bs, Hostels available all over Glasgow, to say that you're spoiled for choice would not be an exaggeration. If you are looking for something a bit more historical, then see; Chapter 9 – Stay in a Castle or Stately Home.
We stayed in the following hotels on our last few trips and can recommend all of them (I have stayed in others, but it was some time ago, so don't feel I can recommend them);

Premier Inn, Milngavie(7 miles North Square)

- Modern hotel situated close to Loch Lomond and the start of the "West Highland Way" hiking trail. We stayed here the night prior to hiking the "West Highland Way."
  www.premierinn.com

Oak Tree Inn(22 miles North from George Square)

- Hotel overlooking Loch Lomond with its own Brewery.
  www.theoaktreeinn.co.uk
  Balmaha.

The Inn on Loch Lomond(35 miles from George Square)

- Hotel overlooking Loch Lomond. We stayed in the Beach Ben Vane room, which had a four-poster bed and was right down on the Loch away from the main hotel.
  www.innonlochlomond.co.uk
  Inverbeg, Alexandria.

Rowardennan Hotel(30 miles North fromGeorge Square)

- We spent the night here at the Hotel (Built around 1696) overlooking Loch Lomond. The road ends shortly after the hotel and you have to turn around and come back.
  www.rowardennanhotel.co.uk
  Rowardennan.

The Ardlui Hotel (50 milesNorth from George Square)

- Overlooking Loch Lomond, the Hotel, Marina & Holiday Home Park is owned and operated by the Squires Family since 1959.
  https://ardlui.com
  Ardlui.

Things to do and see

I have used George Square (City Center) as my anchor point for distances to the various sites listed below as George Square is hard to miss for first time visitors to Glasgow due to its central location just outside of Queens Street Train Station.
Glasgow is split in two by the river Clyde.
There are many indoor places (Museums, Art Galleries etc.) that I'd recommend you leave until towards the end of your trip.
That way if you get a rainy day, you can visit one or more of them, if you are very fortunate with the weather, they will be waiting for you to get to them.
If you are a movie fan, there have been many films shot in Glasgow and many TV series (including Outlander). Should you wish to see the locations of your favorite movies or TV series, go to;
https://peoplemakeglasgow.com/top-film-and-tv-locations-in-glasgow
A great resource for fans.

Celtic Connections

- This is the largest winter festival of its kind. Each year there are over 300 events around the city, including ceilidhs (traditional Scottish dance event), talks, art shows, workshops and concerts. Held mid-January to early February each year.
  www.celticconnections.com

Glasgow Film Festival

- From new blockbusters to avant-garde arthouse, live talks and rare cult classics. Held from late February to early March. https://glasgowfilm.org

North from Glasgow City Center

Outdoor Pursuits Scotland(2 miles North from George Square)

- Canyoning, Funyaking, Gorge walking, River Boogieboarding, Paddle sports, White Water Rafting.
  www.outdoorpursuitsscotland.co.uk
  75 N Canal Bank Street, Glasgow.

Bearsden and Milngavie Highland Games
(7 miles North from George Square)

- Held in early-June each year. Tossing the Caber, Highland dancing, Athletics, and Pipe bands.
  www.bearsdenmilngaviehighlandgames.com
  Burnbrae the Home of West Rugby, Glasgow Rodd, Milngavie.

Stirling (Pop. 36,000)
(26 miles North and East from George Square)

Stirling is a good option to staying in Edinburgh or Glasgow being situated roughly half-way between the two and close to Stirling, there are good bus and rail links to Edinburgh and Glasgow. I will now use Stirling as a base for distances to sites/attractions.

- Hotels, B&Bs, Food, Drink, Car Hire, Buses, Taxis, Shops, ATMs/Banks, Museum, **Gas (petrol) & Charging Stations**.

Stirling Castle

- 12th century castle built on an extinct volcano. The castle has seen many kings, queens and battles.
  www.stirlingcastle.scot
  Castle Esplanade.

Church of the Holy Rood

- Beautiful 15th century church with impressive stained glass and crowning place of James the 6th of Scotland.
  www.holyrude.org
  St John Street.

Smith Art Gallery and Museum

- Displaying local history and rotating exhibits.
  www.smithartgalleryandmuseum.co.uk
  40 Albert Place.

North from Stirling Castle

Stirling Bridge(1-mile North from Stirling Castle)

- 15th century stone bridge that replaced the wooden bridge that saw the battle of Stirling Bridge in 1297, where William Wallace and Sir Andrew Moray led the Scottish army to victory over the English.
  www.historicenvironment.scot
  River Forth.

National Wallace monument(2 miles North from Stirling Castle)

- Monument to William Wallace, see the Wallace sword and take in the stunning views over the river Forth valley.
  www.nationalwallacemonument.com
  Abbey Craig, Hillfoots Road.

Bridge of Allan Highland Games (4 miles North from Stirling Castle)

- Held in Early-August each year. Tossing the Caber, Highland dancing, Athletics, and Pipe bands.
  http://bofagames.com
  Strathallan Games Park, Bridge of Allan.

Broomhall Castle Hotel(6 miles North from Stirling Castle)

- Built in 1836 in the style of Balmoral castle. With views of Stirling Castle and the Wallace Monument.
  www.broomhallcastle.co.uk
  Long Row, Menstrie.

Alva Highland Games (7 miles North from Stirling Castle)

- Held in Mid-July each year. Tossing the Caber, Highland dancing, Athletics, and Pipe bands.
  http://alva.ukctest.co.uk
  Johnstone Park, Alva.

Deanston Distillery(8 miles North from Stirling Castle)

- Pronunciation: Dean-stin
- Name Origin: Gaelic - "The hill fort."
- Established: 1966.
- Location: Teith Road, Deanston, Doune.
- Region: Highland.
- Visitor Center/Tours: Go to website for information.
- Website:www.deanstonmalt.com

Bridge of Allan Highland Games (4 miles North from Stirling Castle)

- Held in Early-August each year. Tossing the Caber, Highland dancing, Athletics, and Pipe bands.
  http://bofagames.com
  Strathallan Games Park, Bridge of Allan.

Alva Highland Games (7 miles North from Stirling Castle)

- Held in Mid-July each year. Tossing the Caber, Highland dancing, Athletics, and Pipe bands.
  http://alva.ukctest.co.uk
  Johnstone Park, Alva.

Deanston Distillery(8 miles North and West from Stirling Castle)

- Pronunciation: Dean-stin
- Name Origin: Gaelic - "The hill fort."
- Established: 1966.
- Location: Teith Road, Deanston, Doune.
- Region: Highland.
- Visitor Center/Tours: Go to website for information.
- Website:www.deanstonmalt.com

Doune Castle (8 miles North and West from Stirling Castle)

- Robert Stewart, the 1st Duke of Albany and Governor of Scotland acquired the castle in 1361, when he married Margaret Graham, Countess of Menteith.
  www.historicenvironment.scot
  Castle Hill, Doune.

Tullibardine Distillery(16 miles North from Stirling Castle)

- Pronunciation: Tulli-Bar-Dine

- Name Origin: Gaelic - "Hill of warning."

- Established: 1949.

- Location: Stirling Street, Blackford, Auchterarder.

- Region: Highland.

- Visitor Center/Tours: Go to website for information.

- Website:www.tullibardine.com

South from Stirling Castle

Bannockburn Battle Site and visitor center

(4 miles South from Stirling Castle)

- On the 23 and 24 June 1314 King Robert the Bruce led a Scottish army to victory over a larger English army led by King Edward the 2nd.
  www.nts.org.uk/visit/places/bannockburn
  Bannockburn, Stirling.

East from Stirling Castle

Cambuskenneth Abbey (1-mile East from Stirling Castle)

- Apart from the foundations of the 13th century Abbey, all that remains is the Bell Tower and the graves of King James the 3rd and his wife Queen Margaret of Denmark.
  Ladysneuk Road, Cambuskenneth

Stirling Highland Games (3 miles East from Stirling Castle)

- Held in Mid-August each year. Tossing the Caber, Highland dancing, Athletics, and Pipe bands.
  www.stirlinghighlandgames.com
  Stirling Games Field, Royal Stuart Way, Stirling.

Airth Highland Games(9 miles East and South from Stirling Castle)

- Held in Late-July each year. Tossing the Caber, Highland dancing, Athletics, and Pipe bands.
  www.airthgames.co.uk
  Airth.

Airth Castle (10 miles East and South from Stirling Castle)

- Once owned by the family of Robert the Bruce and dating back to the 14th century.
  www.airthcastlehotel.com
  Airth.

West from Stirling Castle

Kinlochard Highland Games(24 miles West from Stirling Castle)

- Held in Late-July each year. Tossing the Caber, Highland dancing, Athletics, and Pipe bands.
  www.kinlochard.org
  Kinlochard, Stirling.

North from Glasgow City Center

Loch Lomond

Loch Lomond is the largest lake by surface area in Great Britain, and the second largest lake by volume in Great Britain, after Loch Ness. There are a number of towns and villages around the loch, I have listed the main ones below.

Alexandria (Pop. 13,000)

(18 miles North and West from George Square)

Situated at the Southern end of Loch Lomond. There are good bus and rail links to Glasgow. Alexandria, Balloch, and Jamestown meld into each other, so you can easily walk all three of them.

- Hotels, B&Bs, Food, Drink, Car Hire, Buses, Taxis, Shops, ATMs/Banks, Museum, **Gas (petrol) & Charging Stations**.

Loch Lomond Distillery

- Pronunciation: Lock-Low-mond.
- Name Origin: For the Loch.
- Established: 1964.
- Location: Bowie Road, Alexandria.
- Region: Highland.
- Visitor Center/Tours: Go to website for information.
- Website:www.lochlomondgroup.com

Balloch

(Pronounced Bal – Ok)
(2 miles North of Alexandria)

Situated at the Southern end of Loch Lomond. I will be using Balloch for distances around Loch Lomond. With Aquarium, water sports, loch cruises, golf, shopping, and sightseeing.

- Hotels, B&Bs, Food, Drink, Car Hire, Buses, Taxis, Shops, ATMs/Banks, Medical Center, **Gas (petrol) & Charging Stations**.

Loch Lomond Highland Games

- Held in Early-July each year. Tossing the Caber, Highland dancing, Athletics, and Pipe bands.
  www.llhgb.com
  Moss O Balloch Park, Balloch.

Heading up the East side of Loch Lomond

Large sections of the East side have no roads alongside the Loch, but there is a road from Balmaha to Rowardennan that affords great views.

Balloch Castle and Country Park(1-mile East and North fromBalloch)

- The castle is not open to visitors, but there is a great deal to do in the 200-acre park. The Park is one of the finest public spaces in the West of Scotland with fantastic views over Loch Lomond and plenty of things to see and do.
  www.lovelochlomond.com
  20 Park Avenue, Balloch, Alexandria.

Devil's Pulpit (9 miles East from Balloch)

- Small, but stunning gorge in Fiddich Valley. https://thedevilspulpit.wpcomstaging.com *Blair Court, A890 Dumgoyne.*

Drymen Village

(Pronounced Dri (as in drink) - men
(9 miles East from Balloch)

We stopped here at the "Clachan Inn" (Established 1734) for a drink after the first day of the West Highland Way hike. Seemingly the famous Scottish outlaw Rob Roy's sister was owner at one point.

- Hotels, Food, Drink, Shops, ATM, Medical Center, Post Office, **Gas (petrol)**.

Glengoyne Distillery (12 miles East from Balloch)

- Pronunciation: Glen-goyne.
- Name Origin: Gaelic - "Valley of the Wild Geese."
- Established: 1833.
- Location: Dumgoyne, Killearn near Glasgow.
- Region: Highland.
- Visitor Center/Tours: Go to website for information.
- Website:www.glengoyne.com

Balmaha

(12 miles East and North from Balloch)

You can go on boat trips to some of the islands from here and if you feel up to it, a hike to the top of Conic hill gives breath-taking views of Loch Lomond and the highlands.

- Hotels, B&Bs, Food, Drink, Shops. We spent the night here at the Oak Tree Inn overlooking Loch Lomond.

Rowardennan Hotel(19 miles North from Balloch)

- We spent the night here at the Hotel (Built around 1696) overlooking Loch Lomond. The road ends shortly after the hotel and you have to turn around and come back.
  www.rowardennanhotel.co.uk
  Rowardennan.

Inversnaid Hotel(33 miles North from Balloch)

- The hotel was once a hunting lodge for the Duke of Montrose. To get there, the road loops out from the loch and swings around ending at the Hotel and you have to turn around and come back. We have not stayed here, although we did stop for lunch on our hike, and now understand why it was one of Queen Victoria's favorite places to have lunch. The hotel sits right on Loch Lomond and the views are fantastic.
  www.rowardennanhotel.co.uk
  Rowardennan.

Heading up the West side of Loch Lomond

The road follows the Western shoreline of Loch Lomond.

Cameron House Hotel (2 miles Northformalism)

- Baronial Mansion sitting on the "Bonnie, Bonnie banks" of Loch Lomond.
  www.cameronhouse.co.uk
  Alexandria, Loch Lomond.

Loch Lomond Sea Planes (2 miles North from Balloch)

- Flying tours over the West Coast and fights to Oban and the isle of Bute.
  www.lochlomondseaplanes.com
  Duck Bay, Alexandria.

Luss Village

(9 miles North from Balloch)

Picturesque village used as the location for the TV series “Take the High Road.”

- Hotels, B&Bs, ATM, Food, Drink, Post Office and Shops.

Luss (Loch Lomond) Highland Gathering

- Held in Early-July each year. Tossing the Caber, Highland dancing, Athletics, and Pipe bands.
  www.lusshighlandgames.co.uk
  Luss, Loch Lomond.

Tarbet Village

(17 miles North from Balloch)

The West Highland Railway passes the village and offers services to Glasgow, Oban or Fort William.

- Hotels, B&Bs, ATM, Food, Drink, Post Office and Shops with cruises available on the Loch.

N

W E

S

South from Glasgow City Center& South of the River Clyde

Scotland Street School Museum(2 miles South from George Square)

- Opened in 1906 and designed by Charles Rennie Mackintosh. Telling the story of 100 years of education in Scotland.
  www.glasgowlife.org.uk
  225 Scotland Street, Glasgow.

The People's Palace (Free)
(2 miles South East from George Square)

- On Glasgow Green. Objects, photographs, prints and film which give a unique view into how Glaswegians lived, worked and played in years gone by to the present day.
  www.glasgowlife.org.uk
  Glasgow Green, Templeton Street.

Sherbrooke Castle Hotel(4 miles South from George Square)

- Lovely Baronial House built in 1896, with restaurant and bar.
  https://sherbrookecastlehotel.com
  11 Sherbrooke Avenue, Bellahouston.

Pollock House(5 miles South West from George Square)

- Edwardian Country house in the heart of Glasgow.
  www.nts.org.uk
  2060 Pollokshaws Road, Bellahouston.

Crookston Castle(6 miles South West from George Square)

- Ruined castle built around 1400, offering views over the city.
  www.historicenvironment.scot
  170 Brockburn Road.

Carmunnock Highland Games (8 miles South from George Square)

- Held Late-May each year. Tossing the Caber, Highland dancing, Athletics, and Pipe bands.
  http://blackfordhighlandgames.co.uk
  Carmunnock, Glasgow.

National Museum of Rural Life(8 miles South from George Square)

- Learn about the people and how they worked the land, with the largest collection of farm machinery in Scotland.
  www.nms.ac.uk/rural
  Wester Kittochside Philipshill Road East Kilbride.

Crossbasket CastleHotel(8 miles South East from George Square)

- This 17th century castle has been transformed into one of Scotland's most luxurious hotels.
  www.crossbasketcastle.com
  Stoneymeadow Road, East Kilbride.

East from Glasgow City Center

Glasgow Green (1-mile from George Square)

- 136-acre park, Glasgow's oldest. Home to the World Pipe Band Competition.
  www.glasgow.gov.uk/glasgowgreen
  Greendyke Street, Saltmarket.

World Pipe Band Competition (1-mile from George Square)

- World Pipe Band Competition held each year in August and hosting pipe bands from all over the World.
  www.theworlds.co.uk
  Greendyke Street, Saltmarket.

Provand's Lordship (Free)
(1-mile East from George Square)

- Built in 1471 and one of only four surviving medieval buildings in Glasgow. The "auld hoose" is furnished with a fine selection of 17th-century historic furniture and royal portraits.
  www.glasgowlife.org.uk
  3 Castle Street.

Glasgow Cathedral (Free)
(1-mile East from George Square)

- The first stone-built Glasgow Cathedral was dedicated in the presence of King David I in 1136. The present building was consecrated in 1197. The Cathedral has never been unroofed, and the worship of God has been carried out within its walls for more than 800 years.
  www.glasgowcathedral.org
  Castle Street.

Glasgow Necropolis (Free)
(1-mile East from George Square)

- Guided walking tours are available, (or you can take a leisurely stroll) of this 37-acre cemetery full of wonderful architecture, sculpture and fascinating stories relating to the 50,000 people remembered here. As a charity, donations are appreciated and are used for restoration work.
  www.glasgownecropolis.org
  Castle Street.

Summerlee Museum of Scottish Industrial Life
(Free) (10 miles East from George Square)

- Social history, interactive displays and play park.
  https://culturenl.co.uk
  Heritage Way, Coatbridge.

Bothwell Castle (12 miles East from George Square)

- Built in the late 1200s and constantly fought over and held by the English and Scots at various times.
  www.historicenvironment.scot
  Castle Avenue, Uddingston.

Shotts Highland Games (24 miles East from George Square)

- Held early-June each year. Tossing the Caber, Highland dancing, Athletics, and Pipe bands.
  www.shottshighlandgames.org.uk
  Hannah Park, Shotts.

Falkirk (Pop. 35,000)

(24 miles East from George Square)

Falkirk is a good option to stay, being situated roughly half-way between Edinburgh and Glasgow with good bus and rail links to both and also close to Stirling.

- Hotels, B&Bs, Food, Drink, Car Hire, Buses, Taxis, Shops, ATMs/Banks, Museum, **Gas (petrol) & Charging Stations**.

Callendar House

- 14th century, French chateau style Country House.
  www.visitfalkirk.com
  Callendar Road, Falkirk.

The Falkirk Wheel

- The world's only rotating boat lift, joining the Forth and Clyde canal with the Union canal. You can take a boat trip and get lifted up (35 meters) to the next canal.
  www.scottishcanals.co.uk
  Lime Road, Falkirk.

Scottish Segway Center

- Off-road guided Segway tours around some of the best sites in Scotland. Guides will take you through winding woodland paths and off-road tracks to discover breathtaking views and historic scenery including the remains of a UNESCO World Heritage, Rough Castle, an ancient Roman Fortress.
  https://scottishsegway.com
  The Falkirk Wheel, Falkirk.

The Kelpies

- The world's only rotating boat lift, joining the Forth and Clyde canal with the Union canal. You can take a boat trip and get lifted up (35 meters) to the next canal.
  www.thehelix.co.uk
  Visitor Centre The Helix.

Powfoulis House Hotel(26 miles East from George Square)

- Country Manor house, that was in the hands of the Bruce family for 10 generations.
  www.powfoulis.com
  Bothkennar, Falkirk.

West from Glasgow City Center& North of the Clyde River

Glasgow Botanic Gardens(Free)
(2 miles West and North of the river from George Square)

- Botanic gardens.
  www.glasgowbotanicgardens.com
  50 Pacific Quay.

University of Glasgow (Free)
(2 miles West from George Square)

- Guided and self-guided tours are available. Founded in 1451, the University is the fourth oldest in the UK and the second oldest in Scotland and has more listed buildings than any other university in the UK. A short walk from Kelvingrove Art Gallery and Museum.
  www.gla.ac.uk
  University of Glasgow, 82 Hillhead Street.

Huntarian Art Museum (Free)
(2 miles West from George Square)

- Scotland's oldest public Museum opened in 1807. A short walk from Kelvingrove Art Gallery and Museum.
  www.gla.ac.uk/hunterian
  University of Glasgow, 82 Hillhead Street.

Huntarian Zoology Museum (Free)
(2 miles West from George Square)

- Displays of the earth's diverse animals. A short walk from Kelvingrove Art Gallery and Museum.
  www.gla.ac.uk/hunterian
  University of Glasgow, 82 Hillhead Street.

Kelvingrove Art Gallery and Museum (Free)
(2 miles West from George Square)

- With 22 galleries that showcase everything from art to animals, Ancient Egypt to Charles Rennie Mackintosh and so much more. A short walk from the University of Glasgow and Huntarian Museums.
  www.glasgowlife.org.uk
  Argyle Street.

Riverside Museum (Free)
(3 miles West from George Square)

- Scotland's museum of transport and travel.
www.glasgowlife.org.uk
100 Pointhouse Road, Govan.

Clydeside Distillery(5 miles West from George Square)

- Pronunciation: Clyde-side

- Name Origin: Built on the side of the Clyde river.

- Established: 2017.

- Location: The Old Pump House, Queen's Dock, 100 Stobcross Road, Glasgow.

- Region: Lowland.

- Visitor Center/Tours: Go to website for information.

- Website:www.theclydeside.com

Titan Clydebank (7 miles West from George Square)

- The largest cantilever crane ever built (1907) and used to build ships such as the Queen Mary, Queen Elizabeth, Queen Elizabeth 2 (QE2) and the Royal Yacht Britannia. Now opened as a visitor attraction.
  www.titanclydebank.com
  Garth Drive off Cart Street, Queens Quay, Clydebank.

Auchentoshan Distillery(13 miles West from George Square)

- Pronunciation: Ok-En-Tosh-en.
- Name Origin: Gaelic - "Corner of the field."
- Established: 1823.
- Location: Clydebank.
- Region: Lowland.
- Visitor Center/Tours: Go to website for information.
- Website:www.auchentoshan.com

Dumbarton Castle(15 miles West from George Square)

- The medieval castle was built around 1220 by King Alexander II to defend against the Vikings. www.historicenvironment.scot

Helensburgh (Pop. 14,000)

(31 miles West from George Square)

Small seaside town, a few miles away from the Faslane Naval base. Charles Rennie Mackintosh designed a stylish mansion here, John Logie Baird (1888-1946) the inventor of television was born and grew up here and John Muir the father of the American National Park system boarded a boat here to take him to America. I also lived here while serving in the Navy.
Good train and bus services.

- Hotels, B&Bs, Food, Drink, Car Hire, Buses, Taxis, Shops, ATMs/Banks, Museum, **Gas (petrol) & Charging Stations**.

Hill House

- Built in 1902-04 this house was designed by renowned Scottish architect Charles Rennie Mackintosh. The house includes furniture designed by Mackintosh and his wife. The attic rooms are available to rent as a holiday flat, and there is a tearoom and shop. The gardens have been restored to the original design and are free to visit all year.
  www.nts.org.uk/visit/places/the-hill-house
  Upper Colquhoun Street, Helensburgh.

Helensburgh and Lomond Highland Games

- Held early-June each year. Tossing the Caber, Highland dancing, Athletics, and Pipe bands.
  www.helensburghandlomondgames.co.uk
  Rugby Ground, Helensburgh.

Rosneath Peninsula Highland Games

(13 miles West from Helensburgh)

- Held in Mid-July each year. Tossing the Caber, Highland dancing, Athletics, and Pipe bands.
  www.rosneathgames.co.uk
  Rosneath, Helensburgh.

West from Glasgow City Center& South of the Clyde River

Glasgow Science Center (2 miles West from George Square)

- Science Museum with interactive exhibits.
  www.glasgowsciencecentre.org
  50 Pacific Quay.

Glasgow Distillery (8 miles West from George Square)

- Pronunciation: Glass-Go
- Name Origin: Named for the city.
- Established: 2014.
- Location: 8 Deanside Road, Glasgow.
- Region: Lowland.
- Visitor Center/Tours: At time of writing, the distillery has no tours, but expects to have tours soon. Go to website for updates.
- Website:www.glasgowdistillery.com

Paisley Thread Mill Museum(9 miles West from George Square)

- Telling the story of Thread Making in Paisley from its origin in 1722 to the close of the last mill in 1993.
  Open on Wednesday and Saturday afternoons, all year round.
  https://paisleythreadmill.co.uk
  12 Seedhill Road, Paisley.

Paisley Abbey(11 miles West from George Square)

- Founded in 1163 and still a working church.
  www.paisleyabbey.org.uk
  575 Cotton Street, Paisley.

Newark Castle (23 miles West from George Square)

- The castle was built circa 1478 and was home to the Maxwell family.
  www.historicenvironment.scot
  Castle Road, Port Glasgow.

Gourock(Pop. 12,000)

(29 miles West from George Square)

For Ferries to Kilgreggan, Hunter's Quay and Dunoon. Well served by trains and buses from Glasgow.

- Hotels, B&Bs, Food, Drink, Car Hire, Buses, Taxis, Shops, ATMs/Banks, **Gas (petrol) & Charging Stations**.

Gourock Highland Games

- Held early-May each year at Battery Park. Tossing the Caber, Highland dancing, Athletics, and Pipe bands.
  www.inverclyde.gov.uk
  Battery Park Sports Pavilion, Eldon Street, Greenock.

Kilwinning Abbey(31 miles West from George Square)

- Ruins of a 12th century Abbey.
  www.historicenvironment.scot
  65 Main Street, Kilwinning.

Castle LevanHotel(32 miles West from George Square)

- Castle Levan was built circa 1457. B&B accommodation in 2 guest bedchambers.
  www.castle-levan.com
  Gourock.

Largs(Pop. 12,000)

(34 miles West from George Square)

Now a seaside resort, but back in 1263 this was where Viking power in Scotland was broken, at the Battle of Largs. Largs is the ferry port for the short crossing to the Isle of Great Cumbrae, and a good base for exploring Ayrshire.

- Hotels, B&Bs, Food, Drink, Car Hire, Buses, Taxis, Shops, ATMs/Banks, **Gas (petrol) & Charging Stations**. For Ferries to the Isle of Cumbrae. Well served by trains and buses from Glasgow.

Largs Viking Festival

- Held annually in the last week of August and the first week of September in the town of Largs. To commemorate the Battle of Largs, the last ever Viking invasion on British soil. https://largsvikingfestival.org

Vikingar

- Historical and action-packed Viking experience. https://kaleisure.com/location/vikingar

Wemyss Bay(34 miles West from George Square)

- Village with ferry terminal. For Ferries to Rothesay Isle of Bute. Well served by trains and buses from Glasgow.

Ardrossan

(35 miles West from George Square)

For Ferries to the Isle of Arran and Campbeltown on the Kintyre Peninsula. Well served by trains and buses from Glasgow.

- Hotels, B&Bs, Food, Drink, Car Hire, Buses, Taxis, Shops, ATMs/Banks, **Gas (petrol) & Charging Stations**.

Ardrossan Highland Games

- Held in early-June each year. Tossing the Caber, Highland dancing, Athletics, and Pipe bands.
  www.ardrossanhighlandgames.org.uk
  Memorial Field Pavilion, Sorbie Road, Ardrossan.

Chapter 3

Southern Scotland

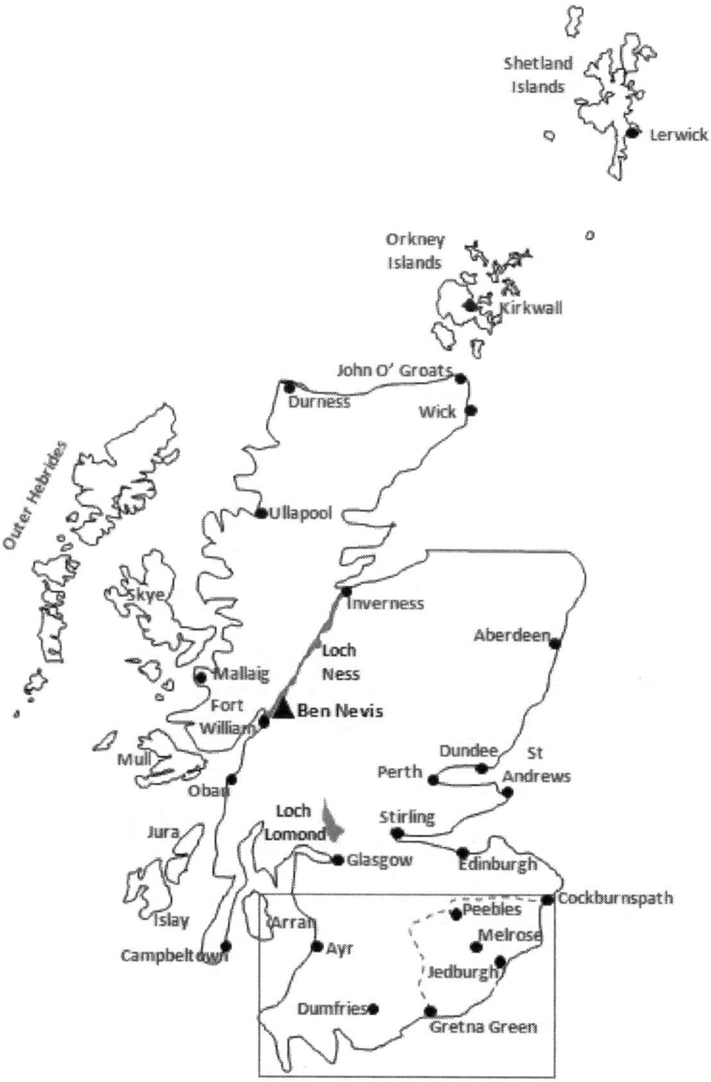

I have divided Southern Scotland into two areas, starting with the South East (Borders region, to the right of the dotted line) and then the South West region (to the left of the dotted line).

The South East

(The Borders)
Down South from Edinburgh

Peebles (Pop. 8,000)

(23 miles South from the Scott Monument in Edinburgh)

I have started with Peebles as it is the first town in the Borders region you will come to when heading South from Edinburgh and will be using it as a base for distances to sites/places in the area.

- Hotels, B&Bs, Food, Drink, Car Hire, Buses, Taxis, Shops, ATMs/Banks, Museum, **Gas (petrol) & Charging Stations**.

Neidpath Castle Hotel(1-mile West from Peebles)

- Stay in a 16th Century Castle.
  www.neidpathcastle.com
  Neidpath Castle, Peebles.

Traquair House Hotel(7 miles South from Peebles)

- Scotland's oldest inhabited house. Originally owned by the kings of Scotland, as a hunting lodge. Subsequently the home of the Earls of Traquair.
  The on-site museum documents the extensive history, including a visit from Mary Queen of Scots. It is well known as the oldest inhabited home in Scotland and is less than an hour from Edinburgh.
  https://www.traquair.co.uk
  Traquair House, Traquair, Innerleithen.

Galashiels(Pop. 15,000)

(19 miles East from Peebles)

Historically a major textile and commercial center for Southern Scotland. Gala (as it is commonly referred to) is the location of Herriot Watt University's School of Textiles and Design.

- Hotels, B&Bs, Food, Drink, Car Hire, Buses, Taxis, Shops, ATMs/Banks, Museum, **Gas (petrol) & Charging Stations**.

Old Gala House

- Dating back to 1583 and once home to the Lairds of Galashiels with over 400 years of history, a museum and gallery telling the story of the town and its people.
  www.liveborders.org.uk
  Old Gala House, Scott Cresent, Galashiels.

Abbottsford House & Hotel(3 miles South from Galashiels)

- Abbottsford house, home to Sir Walter Scott.
  www.scottsabbotsford.com
  Abbotsford House, Melrose.

Monteviot House(15 miles South from Galashiels)

- Originally built as a lodge by the 1st Marquis of Lothian in the early 18th century.
  www.monteviot.com
  Jedburgh.

Monteath Mausoleum(13 miles South from Galashiels)

- The monument is open to walkers and cyclists every day. A key is available to see inside the Crypt.
  Vehicle access and a guide are available only on Open Days (see website for details).
  www.friendsofthemonteathmausoleum.org.uk
  A68, Jedburgh.

Floors Castle(15 miles East from Galashiels)

- Built for the 1st Duke of Roxburghe in 1721, and still home to Roxburghe family with the 11th duke currently residing there.
  www.floorscastle.com
  Roxburghe Estates Office, Kelso.

Mellerstain House (14 miles West from Galashiels)

- Stately home built in 1778.
  www.mellerstain.com
  Mellerstain House, Gordon.

Selkirk(Pop.6,000)

(22 miles South/East from Peebles)

William Wallace was proclaimed Overlord of Scotland in the town's Forest Kirk and Sir Walter Scott served here as Sheriff for 33 years.

- Hotels, B&Bs, Food, Drink, Buses, Taxis, Shops, ATMs/Banks, Museum, **Gas (petrol) & Charging Stations**.

Halliwell's House Museum

- 18th century house, featuring the industrial heritage of the town.
  www.liveborders.org.uk
  Market Place, Selkirk.

Lochcarron of Scotland Visitor center

- The largest remaining working textile mill in the heart of the Scottish Borders.
  www.lochcarron.co.uk
  Waverley Mill, Dunsdale Road, Selkirk.

Selkirk Common Riding

- Held annually in early-June and dating back over 400 years to the time of the "Burleymen", Burgh Law men who had the task of ensuring no one was encroaching on the town's common lands. Also remembered is the return of only one man from the battle of Flodden in 1513 after 80 men from Selkirk followed James IV into battle. That one man (Fletcher) returned, weary and wounded but bearing a captured English flag which he raised aloft and then cast to the ground. The Riding of the Marches lasts about 4½ hours and the riders return to the Market Place. Celebrations continue into the next day with horse racing, and professional games.
  https://returntotheridings.co.uk/selkirk-common-riding

Bowhill House(4 miles West from Selkirk)

- Built over 200 years ago this large country house and estate sits in the Ettrick Forest.
  www.bowhillhouse.co.uk
  Bowhill House, Selkirk.

Aikwood Tower Hotel(5 miles West from Selkirk)

- Tower House hotel. The first mention of Aikwood comes in the Lord Treasurer of Scotland's accounts of 1455. www.aikwoodtower.com *Aikwood Tower, Selkirk.*

Melrose (Pop. 2,000)

(25 miles East from Peebles)

There has been a settlement here for thousands of years and the Romans established a fort here called Trimontium. Melrose is world famous (if you like rugby), with the "Melrose sevens" competition held here each year since 1883, with teams from all over the world competing.

- Hotels, B&Bs, Food, Drink, Buses, Taxis, Shops, ATMs/Banks, Museum, Hospital, **Gas (petrol) & Charging Stations**.

Borders Abbeys Way

- A circular hike connecting the historic Border towns and their famous Abbeys (Dryburgh, Jedburgh, Kelso &Melrose).
  Distance: 64.4mi/103km
  Duration: 4 days
  Height Gain: 990ft/300m
  www.bordersabbeysway.com

Melrose Abbey

- David the 1st founded Scotland's first Cistercian monastery here in 1136. King Robert the Bruce's heart is buried here.
  www.historicenvironment.scot
  Abbey Street, Melrose.

Trimontium Museum

- Showcasing Roman occupation and local history.
  www.trimontium.co.uk
  The Ormiston, Market Square, Melrose.

Dryburgh Abbey(8 miles East from Melrose)

- The abbey was established by Premonstratensian canons in 1150. Sir Walter Scott the famous Scottish novelist is buried here.
  www.historicenvironment.scot
  Dryburgh, St Boswells, Melrose.

Dryburgh Abbey Hotel(8 miles East from Melrose)

- Baronial House built in 1845, 1-minute walk from Dryburgh Abbey.
  www.aikwoodtower.com
  Dryburgh Abbey Hotel, St Boswells, Melrose.

Hawick (Pop. 14,000)

(Pronounced Haw – ik)
(32 miles South from Peebles)

In town the monument the "Turning of the Bull" depicts William Rule turning the wild bull as it was charging King Robert the Bruce, thus saving the king's life and beginning the Scottish Clan of Turnbull.

- Hotels, B&Bs, Food, Drink, Buses, Taxis, Shops, ATMs/Banks, Museums, **Gas (petrol) & Charging Stations**.

Borders Textile Tower House

- Museum featuring the region's knitwear and tweed manufacturing history.
www.liveborders.org.uk
1 Tower Knowe, Hawick.

Hawick Museum

- 18th century mansion set in beautiful parkland, now home to the town's museum.
www.liveborders.org.uk
Wilton Lodge Park.

The Borders Distillery

- Pronunciation: The Borders.
- Name Origin: It is situated in the Scottish Borders.
- Established: 2018.
- Location: Hawick, in the Scottish Borders.
- Region: Lowland.
- Visitor Center/Tours: Go to website for information.
- Website:www.thebordersdistillery.com

Mansfield HouseHotel(1-mile East from Hawick)

- Built in the 1800s as a private residence. We haven't stayed here yet, but after stopping for (a huge) Scottish breakfast on our way through Hawick, we agreed that should we come this way again we would stay here.
www.themansfieldhousehotel.co.uk
Weensland Road, Hawick.

Hermitage Castle(Ruin)(16 milesSouth from Hawick)

- The first castle built on this site was started around 1360 and the present castle has stood here for over 400 years. Described as "the guardhouse of the bloodiest valley in Britain."
www.historicenvironment.scot
Newcastleton, Hawick.

Kelso(Pop.6,000)

(37 miles South/East from Peebles)

The town of Kelso existed prior to the creation of Kelso Abbey in 1128. But after the abbey was completed the town really flourished.

- Hotels, B&Bs, Food, Drink, Buses, Taxis, Shops, ATMs/Banks, Hospital, **Gas (petrol) & Charging Stations**.

Borders Abbeys Way

- A circular hike connecting the historic Border towns and their famous Abbeys (Dryburgh, Jedburgh, Kelso & Melrose).
  Distance: 64.4mi/103km
  Duration: 4 days
  Height Gain: 990ft/300m
  www.bordersabbeysway.com

Kelso Abbey

- The abbey was founded 1128 by monks invited by King David the 1st.
  www.historicenvironment.scot
  Kelso.

Smailholm Tower (7 miles West from Kelso)

- 15th-century tower house and laird's residence.
  www.historicenvironment.scot
  Sandyknowe Farm, Kelso.

Coldstream Museum(10 miles East from Kelso)

- Local history and history on the Coldstream Guards Regiment.
  www.liveborders.org.uk
  Coldstream.

Jedburgh(Pop. 4,000)

(37 miles South/East from Peebles)

In the 9th century a church was built in the settlement. In 1118 a priory was founded and in 1138 an Abbey was founded, both of which helped the settlement grow.

- Hotels, B&Bs, Food, Drink, Buses, Taxis, Shops, ATMs/Banks, Museum, **Gas (petrol) & Charging Stations**.

Borders Abbeys Way

- A circular hike connecting the historic Border towns and their famous Abbeys (Dryburgh, Jedburgh, Kelso & Melrose).
  Distance: 64.4mi/103km
  Duration: 4 days
  Height Gain: 990ft/300m
  www.bordersabbeysway.com

Jedburgh Abbey

- Founded in 1138 by King David the 1st for Augustinian monks.
  www.visitscotland.com
  Abbey Bridge End, Jedburgh.

Jedburgh Castle Jail and Museum

- It looks like a castle, but it's really a jail. If you want to know what life was like in an 1820s prison, this is the place to find out.
  www.liveborders.org.uk
  89 Castle Gate, Jedburgh.

Mary Queen of Scots House

- This historic 16th century Tower House tells the story of Mary Queen of Scots and her life.
  www.liveborders.org.uk
  Queen Street, Jedburgh.

Ferniehirst Castle (2 miles South from Jedburgh)

- First built in 1476 and involved in many wars. It has been destroyed and rebuilt. The present house dates back to around 1598. Only open in July
  www.ferniehirst.com
  Oxnam, Jedburgh.

Duns(Pop.3,000)

(45 miles East from Peebles)

The town has its origins in the Iron Age and the remains of an Iron Age fort can still be seen on the summit of Duns Law (hill). The town is first mentioned in a written record in 1179.

- Hotels, B&Bs, Food, Drink, Buses, Taxis, Shops, ATMs/Banks, Museum, **Gas (petrol) & Charging Stations**.

Jim Clark Motorsport Museum

- This museum is a-must for motor racing fans and anyone looking for a great day out. Jim Clark was Scotland's first, and double, Formula One World Champion, Indy 500 winner and one of the greatest racing drivers of all time.
  www.liveborders.org.uk
  Duns.

Duns Castle Hotel(3 miles from Manderston House)

- 14th century castle. (16 miles from Kelso)
  https://dunscastle.co.uk
  Duns.

Manderston House(3 miles from Duns Castle)

- Beautiful Edwardian country house.
  www.manderston.co.uk
  Manderston, Duns.

Marchmont House(6 miles from Duns Castle)

- Open on limited days of the year for tours (you must book in advance).
  https://marchmonthouse.com
  Marchmont Estate, Greenlaw, Duns.

The South West

Down South from Glasgow

West of the M74 Motorway (Freeway)

Kilmarnock(Pop. 46,000)

(24 miles South West from George Square, Glasgow)

I have started with Kilmarnock as it is the first town in the South West Region you will come to when heading South West from Glasgow and will be using it as a base for distances to sites/places in the area. Good rail and bus links.

- Hotels, B&Bs, Food, Drink, Car Hire, Buses, Taxis, Shops, ATMs/Banks, Museum, **Gas (petrol) & Charging Stations**.

Dean Castle and Country park

- The Boyd family built the first castle here around 1350. Superb collections of armor and musical instruments.
  www.britainexpress.com
  Dean Road, Kilmarnock.

Craufurdland Castle Hotel(4 miles North fromKilmarnock)

- Built in the 13th-century and set in a beautiful estate.
  https://craufurdland.co.uk
  Craufurdland Castle, Kilmarnock.

Dundonald Castle (6 miles West from Kilmarnock)

- The main tower was built in the 1370s by King Robert II of Scotland. Now a ruin, but quite substantial.
  www.historicenvironment.scot
  Winehouse Yett, Dundonald.

Dundonald Highland Games (Free)
6 miles West from Kilmarnock)

- Held in late-August each year. Tossing the Caber, Highland dancing, Athletics, and Pipe bands.
  https://dundonald-games.org.uk
  Dundonald Castle, Winehouse Yett, Dundonald.

Ayr (Pop. 47,000)

(15 miles South West from Kilmarnock)

I will now use Ayr (Robert Burns country) as a base for distances to sites/places in the area. "Auld Ayr, wham ne'er a town surpasses, for honest men and bonnie lasses." Quote from Robert Burns poem Tam O' Shanter. Good rail and bus links.

- Hotels, B&Bs, Food, Drink, Car Hire, Buses, Taxis, Shops, ATMs/Banks, Museum, **Gas (petrol) & Charging Stations**.

Cumnock Highland Games (18 miles West from Ayr)

- Held in Late-August each year. Tossing the Caber, Highland dancing, Athletics, and Pipe bands.
  www.facebook.com/CumnockHighland
  Broomfield Park, Auchinleck Road, Cumnock.

Robert Burn's Birthplace Museum(2 miles South from Ayr)

- Birthplace of Scotland's national Bard in the lovely village of Alloway.
  www.nts.org.uk
  Murdoch's Lone, Alloway.

Alloway Kirk (2 miles South from Ayr)

- Old ruined church made famous by Robert Burns in his poem "Tam O' Shanter. 3-minute walk from the Robert Burn's Birthplace Museum.
  www.nts.org.uk
  40 Alloway.

Rozelle House Museum and Galleries(2 miles South from Ayr)

- The first mansion house was finished in 1760 and rebuilt in the 1830s by Archibald Hamilton. Among its collection of art are the 54 paintings of Robert Burns "Tam O' Shanter by Scottish artist Alexander Goudie.
  www.south-ayrshire.gov.uk
  The Cottage, Monument Road.

Crossraguel Abbey(11 miles South from Ayr)

- Ruined early 13th century Abbey.
  www.historicenvironment.scot
  Maybole.

Culzean Castle Hotel(12 miles South from Ayr)

- Beautiful castle perched on top of a cliff and sitting in the heart of Burns country. Open to the public. "The Eisenhower" at Culzean Castle is a small, country house hotel, located on the upper floors of Culzean Castle.
  www.culzean-eisenhower.com
  Maybole.

Scottish Industrial Railway Center(13 miles South east from Ayr)

- "Living museum' where industrial steam and diesel locomotives are restored and can be seen working.
  www.scottishindustrialrailwaycentre.org.uk
  Dunaskin Bridge, Dalmellington Road, Waterside, Patna.

Turnberry Golf Club and Hotel(17 miles South from Ayr)

- The world-famous golf course was opened in 1902 and the hotel in1906.
  www.turnberry.co.uk
  Girvan.

Carrick Lowland Gathering(22 miles South from Ayr)

- Held in early-June each year. Tossing the Caber, Highland dancing, Athletics, and Pipe bands.
  www.girvanattractions.co.uk/lowland-gathering.php
  Victory Park, Girvan.

Glenapp Castle Hotel(35 miles South from Ayr)

- Welcome to Glenapp Castle, an award winning 5-star Castle Hotel.
  www.glenappcastle.com
  Ballantrae, Girvan.

Side trip East from Ayr

Dumfries House &Hotel(14 miles East from Ayr)

- This 18th-century house and estate, set in 2,000 acres, has an unrivalled collection of Chippendale furniture. Open to the public.
  www.dumfries-house.org.uk
  Dumfries House, Cumnock.

Sanquhar Tollbooth Museum(Free)
(35 miles East from Ayr)

- Discover Sanquhar's world famous knitting tradition and the story of the mines and miners of Sanquhar and Kirkconnel.
  www.dumgal.gov.uk
  High Street, Sanquhar.

Drumlanrig Castle(42 miles East from Ayr)

- The Castle is one of the finest examples of 17th Century Renaissance architecture in Scotland set in 90,000 acres and the stunning Dumfriesshire seat of the Duke and Duchess of Buccleuch and Queensberry.
  www.dumgal.gov.uk
  Thornhill.

Stranraer (Pop. 11,000)

(51 miles South from Kilmarnock)

I will now use Stranraer as a base for distances to sites/places in the area. Stranraer has Ferry links to Larne and Belfast in Northern Ireland. Good rail and bus links to Glasgow.

- Hotels, B&Bs, Food, Drink, Car Hire, Buses, Taxis, Shops, ATMs/Banks, Museum, **Gas (petrol) & Charging Stations**.

Castle of St John(Free)

- Medieval tower built around 1500. Variously used as a home, a local court, a military garrison and a prison.
www.dumgal.gov.uk

Stranraer Museum(Free)

- Housed in the Old Town Hall, built in 1776, Step inside and discover Wigtownshire's fascinating past.
www.dumgal.gov.uk

Dunskey Castle Hotel(8 miles South from Stranraer)

- Set in a 2000-acre estate, it is classed as an Edwardian castle, but looks more like a large manor house to me, nonetheless it has luxurious accommodations with panoramic views.
www.dunskey.com
Dunskey Street, Portpatrick.

Side Trip East from Stranraer

Glenluce Abbey (11 miles East from Stranraer)

- Ruined Abbey founded in the late 12th century.
  www.historicenvironment.scot
  Glenluce, Newton Stewart.

Bladnoch (27 miles East from Stranraer)

- Pronunciation: Blad-nok
- Name Origin: Gaelic (Blaidzenoch) - The name of the local river.
- Established: 1817.
- Location: Bladnoch, Galloway.
- Region: Lowland.
- Visitor Center/Tours: Go to website for information.
- Website: https

Cardoness Castle(42 miles East from Stranraer)

- 15th century six-story tower house.
  www.historicenvironment.scot
  Gatehouse of Fleet, Castle Douglas.

Maclellan Castle (50 miles East from Stranraer)

- Sir Thomas MacLellan's tower house, from the late 1500s.
  www.historicenvironment.scot
  Castle Street, Kirkcudbright.

Threave castle(54 miles East from Stranraer)

- Cross the River Dee by boat to this fortress built by Archibald 'the Grim' in 1369 as a stronghold for the Black Douglases.
  www.historicenvironment.scot
  Dumfries, Castle Douglas.

Dundrennan Abbey(56 miles East from Stranraer)

- Mary Queen of Scots spent her last hours in Scotland here at the Abbey (12th-century) in May 1568.
  www.historicenvironment.scot
  Dundrennan, Kirkcudbright.

Dumfries (Pop. 33,000)

(pronounced Dum-freeze)
(73 miles East from Stranraer)

This is the principal town in South West Scotland. I will now use Dumfries as a base for distances to sites/places in the area. Good rail and bus links to Glasgow.

- Hotels, B&Bs, Food, Drink, Car Hire, Buses, Taxis, Shops, ATMs/Banks, Museum, **Gas (petrol) & Charging Stations**.

Robert Burns House(Free)

- The house (now a museum) where he spent the last five years of his life.
  www.dumgal.gov.uk
  Brooms Road, Dumfries.

Devorgilla Bridge(Free)

- 15th Century footbridge over the River Nith. On the west bank the Old Bridge House, built 1660, is now a small free museum.

Dumfries Museum(Free)

- History of the Dumfries and Galloway area.
  www.dgculture.co.uk
  The Observatory, Rotchell Road, Dumfries.

Aviation Museum(3 miles East from Dumfries)

- Aviation museum on an old Royal Airforce Base.
  www.dumfriesaviationmuseum.com
  Former Control Tower Tinwald Downs Road Heathhall Industrial Estate.

Annandale Distillery(17 miles East from Dumfries)

- Pronunciation: Ann-an-dale.
- Name Origin: Named for the region the distillery is situated in.
- Established: 1836, closed 1924, re-opened 2007.
- Location: Annandale.
- Region: Lowland.
- Visitor Center/Tours: Go to website for information.
- Website: https

SpringkellHotel(21 miles East from Dumfries)

- Mansion house dating from 1734, located close to the historic town of Gretna Green. Individual rooms can now be booked on a dinner, bed and breakfast basis.
  www.springkell.com
  Lockerbie.

New Abbey Corn Mill(8 miles South from Dumfries)

- Working 18th-century, water-powered mill.
  www.historicenvironment.scot
  New Abbey, Dumfries.

Sweetheart Abbey(8 miles South from Dumfries)

- Named "Dulce Cor" by the monks in memory of Lady Dervorguilla, who founded the abbey in tribute to her beloved husband, John Balliol.
  www.historicenvironment.scot
  Main Street, New Abbey.

Caerlaverock Castle(9 miles South from Dumfries)

- Unique triangular castle surrounded by a moat.
  www.historicenvironment.scot
  Caerlaverock.

The Devil's Porridge Museum(19 miles South east from Dumfries)

- Commemorating Her Majesties Factory Gretna, the largest munitions factory in the world during the First World War. Almost 12,000 young women had travelled from across Britain to do their bit for the war effort. They were employed to manage the process of mixing the highly volatile 'devil's porridge'. Sherlock Holmes author, Sir Arthur Conan-Doyle coined the phrase 'the Devil's Porridge' after visiting as a War Correspondent and witnessing the Gretna Girls mixing this dangerous mixture.
  www.devilsporridge.org.uk
  Annan Road, Eastriggs.

Gretna Green (Pop. 3,000)

(24 miles South East from Dumfries)

Famous as a wedding venue for over 250 years, a tradition that began when English marriage laws became restrictive, so couples eloped across the border to Scotland. Good rail and bus links to Glasgow.

- Hotels, B&Bs, Food, Drink, Buses, Taxis, Shops, ATMs, Museum, **Gas (petrol) & Charging Stations**.

Famous Blacksmiths Shop

- Shopping and Wedding Venue at the home of Blacksmith's Anvil weddings since 1754.
  www.gretnagreen.com
  Headless Cross, Gretna Green.

Down South from Glasgow

East of the M74 Motorway (Freeway)

Motherwell (Pop. 32,000)

(16 miles South East from Glasgow)

Former iron and steel-making center. I will now use Motherwell as a base for distances to sites/places in the area.
Good rail and bus links to Glasgow.

- Hotels, B&Bs, Food, Drink, Car Hire, Buses, Taxis, Shops, ATMs/Banks, Museum, **Gas (petrol) & Charging Stations**.

Motherwell Cathedral

- Established 1875, tours available.
  www.motherwell-cathedral.org.uk
  31 Coursington Road.

North Lanarkshire Heritage Centre

- Four-star attraction offering visitors a range of facilities and services for an educational or a fun day out.
  https://culturenl.co.uk
  High Road.

Craignethan Castle(11 miles South East from Motherwell)

- Residential tower and artillery fortification built around 1530.
  www.historicenvironment.scot
  Blackwood, Lesmahagow.

New Lanark World Heritage Site(15 miles South East from Motherwell)

- Founded in 1785 with a focus on philanthropy, education and the welfare of the mill worker. This Mill Village became a model for industrial communities across the world in the 19th and 20th centuries.
  www.newlanark.org
  New Lanark Road, Lanark.

Kagyu Samye Ling Tibetan Monastery

(65 miles South East from Motherwell)

- Day visitors are welcome to visit at no charge, all year round. You can visit the temple, stroll around the peace garden and grounds. You can also relax in the Tibetan Tea Rooms, which offers a wide variety of drinks, snacks and small meals. Overnight guest accommodationist also available, see website for details
  www.samyeling.org
  Eskdalemuir.

Lockerbie (Pop. 4,000)

(59 miles South East from Motherwell)

Small town unfortunately best known for the tragic crash of Pan Am flight 103 after a bomb detonated on-board. Rail and bus links to Glasgow.

- Hotels, B&Bs, Food, Drink, Buses, Taxis, Shops, ATMs, **Gas (petrol) & Charging Stations**.

Dryfesdale Lodge

- The Lockerbie Air Disaster Memorial sits within the tranquil setting of the Garden of Remembrance at the far end of Dryfesdale Cemetery. The garden of pretty flower beds and individual memorials is in remembrance to the 270 victims of the bombing. Within the Garden of Remembrance is an imposing slab of dark grey granite, the Lockerbie Air Disaster Memorial, which has all 270 names carved into it.
  https://dryfesdalelodge.co.uk/memorial
  Dumfries Road, Lockerbie.

Chapter 4

The North East

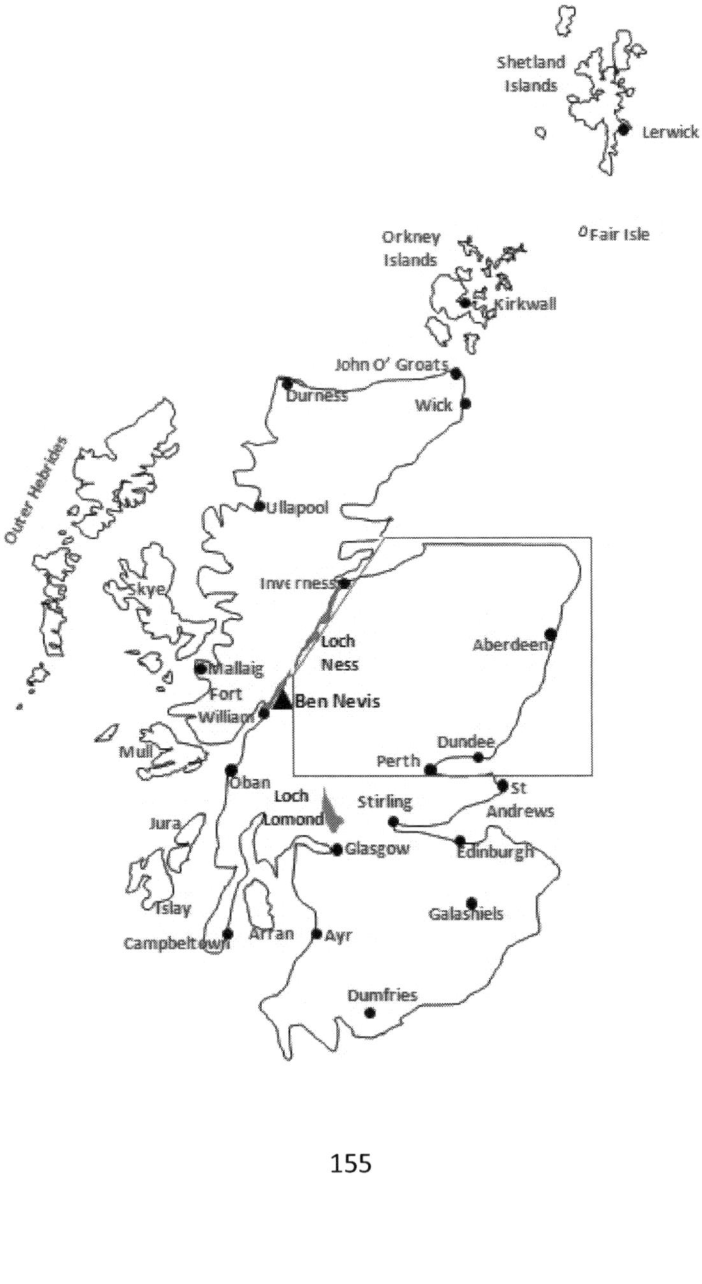

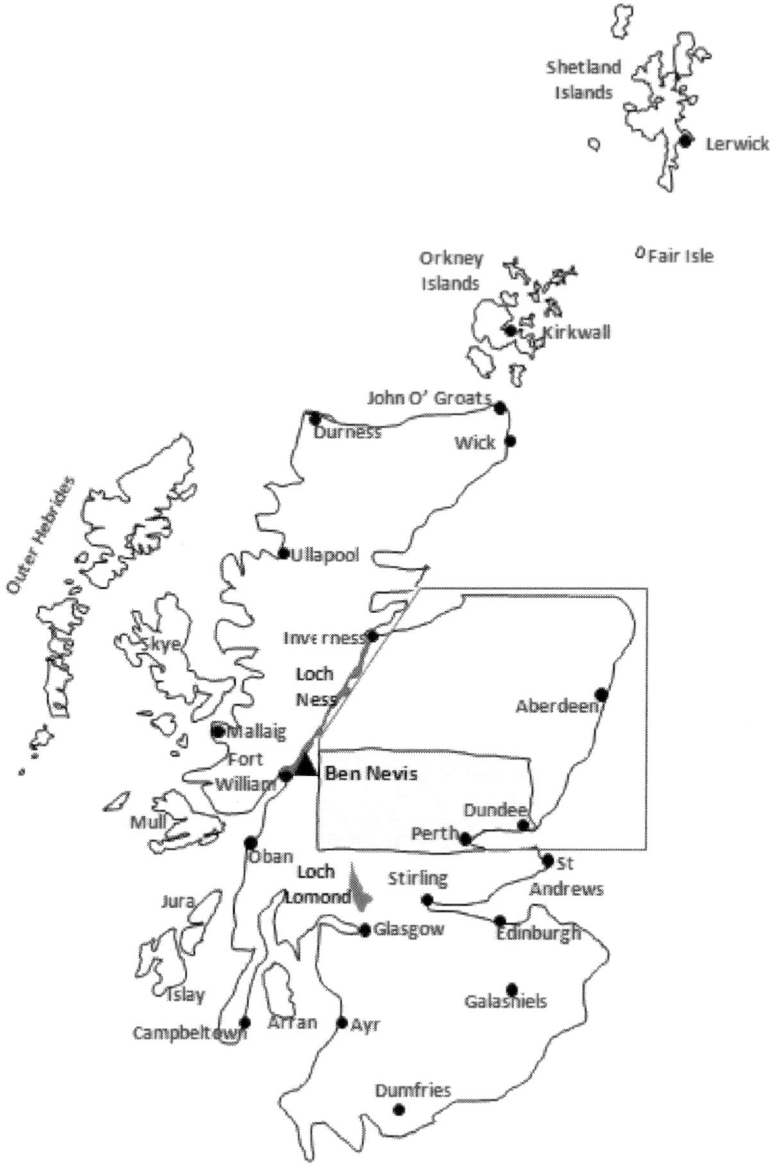

Perth, Dundee, Forfarand Aberfeldy
In the shaded area shown

Perth (Pop. 47,000)

Once Scotland's capital and much favored by King James 1st, with its tall spires and the River Tay flowing through it, it is easy to see why it is known as "The Fair City."
I will now use Perth as a base for distances to sites/places in the area. The Nearest Airport is Dundee Airport (20 miles away).
There are good train and bus services available.

- Hotels, B&Bs, Food, Drink, Car Hire, Buses, Taxis, Shops, ATMs/Banks, Hospital, Museum, **Gas (petrol) & Charging Stations**.

Black watch Castle and Museum

- Spanning centuries this is the history of The Black Watch. From its formation in 1739 to the amalgamation of the Regiment in 2006 The Black Watch has played many pivotal roles in British military history.
  https://theblackwatch.co.uk
  Perth.

Perth Cathedral

- The Cathedral was the first to be built in Britain after the Reformation and was consecrated in 1850. It stands on ground that originally formed part of the Blackfriars Monastery and is dedicated to St. Ninian, the first name we know in the Christian history of Scotland.
  https://perthcathedral.co.uk
  Perth.

Perth Leisure Pool

- Bad weather? Here's an option, with flumes, wild water, slides and an outdoor lagoon.
  www.liveactive.co.uk
  Perth.

Perth Museum and Art Gallery(Free)

- Local history and so much more.
  www.culturepk.org.uk
  Perth.

St John's Kirk

- The first historical reference to a church dedicated to St. John the Baptist in Perth was in 1126, in a grant from King David I. The heart of King Alexander III was buried here in 1286, following his untimely death on the cliffs at Kinghorn in Fife, which precipitated Scotland into the Wars of Independence.
  www.st-johns-kirk.co.uk
  Perth.

Willowgate Activity Center

- Outdoor center with: Aqua Zorbing, Archery, Kayaking, Paddle Boarding & Bike Hire.
  www.willowgateactivitycentre.co.uk
  Stockgreen Lodge, Kinfauns, Perth.

North from Perth

Scone Palace(Pronounced Scoon)
(2 miles North from Perth)

- Traditionally, from the 9th century the Kings of Scotland were crowned here while sat on the "Stone of Destiny" or "Stone of Scone." The present building is a Victorian Mansion, with a replica of the Stone of Destiny - the original is housed in Edinburgh Castle.
  Open April-September.
  https://scone-palace.co.uk
  Perth.

Perth Highland Games (2 miles North from Perth)

- Held mid-August each year at Scone Palace. Tossing the Caber, Highland dancing, Athletics, Pipe bands and Dancing.
  https://perthhighlandgames.co.uk
  Scone Palace, Perth.

Huntingtower Castle(3 miles North from Perth)

- Built around the 1400s, Mary Queen of Scots stayed here in 1565, while on honeymoon with Lord Darnley.
  www.historicenvironment.scot
  Huntingtower.

Stanley Mills(8 miles North from Perth)

- Built in the 1780s and working until 1989, this huge mill produced textiles by harnessed the power of the River Tay.
  www.historicenvironment.scot
  Stanley.

Birnam Highland Games (15 miles North from Perth)

- Held in Late-August each year. Tossing the Caber, Highland dancing, Athletics, and Pipe bands.
  www.birnamhighlandgames.com
  Birnam, Dunkeld.

Blairgowrie & Rattray Highland Games
(16 miles North from Perth)

- Held in Early-September each year. Tossing the Caber, Highland dancing, Athletics, and Pipe bands.
  www.blairgowriehighlandgames.co.uk
  Bogles Field, Essendy Road, Blairgowrie.

Side Trip East of Perth

Elcho Castle(5 miles East from Perth)

- Built around 1560, the fortified mansion is one of Scotland's best-preserved 16th-century tower houses.
  www.historicenvironment.scot
  Castle Wynd, Rhynd.

Side Trip West of Perth

Crieff Highland Games (18 miles West from Perth)

- Held in Mid-August each year. Tossing the Caber, Highland dancing, Athletics, and Pipe bands.
  www.crieffhighlandgathering.com
  Market Park, Crieff.

Knock Castle Hotel(18 miles West from Perth)

- Built in the 1800's as a stately home.
  www.knockcastle.com
  40 Drummond Terrace, Crieff.

Glenturret (19 miles West from Perth)
(The oldest distillery in Scotland).

- Pronunciation: Glen-turr-et.
- Name Origin: Gaelic - "Valley of the little dry stream."
- Established: 1775.
- Location: The Hosh, Crieff.
- Region: Highland.
- Visitor Center/Tours: Go to website for information.
- Website: https

Balquhidder, Lochearnhead &Strathyre Highland Games (37 miles West from Perth)

- Held in Late-July each year. Tossing the Caber, Highland dancing, Athletics, and Pipe bands. http://lochearnheadhighlandgames.co.uk *Lochearnhead.*

Killin Highland Games (45 miles West from Perth)

- Held in Early-August each year. Tossing the Caber, Highland dancing, Athletics, and Pipe bands.
  www.killingames.co.uk
  Breadalbane Park, Killin.

Moirlanich Longhouse(45 miles West from Perth)

- An early 19th century traditional longhouse.
  www.nts.org.uk
  Glen Lochay, Killin.

East from Perth

Dundee (Pop. 150,000)
(22 miles East of Perth)

Dundee used to be an industrial town famous for its Jam and textile mills, also for its cartoons and comics (D C Thomson publishing), "Oor Wullie" and "The Broons" (Newspaper cartoons), the Dandy and the Beano children's comics.
Dundee also has its great cultural icon William McGonagall widely regarded as the world's worst poet. Most of the sights that you would want to see are within walking distance of each other. I will now use Dundee as a base for distances to sites/places in the area.
There are good train and bus services available.
Dundee Airport (3 miles to Dundee)
www.hial.co.uk/dundee-airport

- Hotels, B&Bs, Food, Drink, Car Hire, Buses, Taxis, Shops, ATMs/Banks, Hospital, Museums, **Gas (petrol) & Charging Stations**.

Ancrum Outdoor Center

- Archery, Hill Walking & Climbing, Mountain Biking, Snow Sports, and Water Sports.
  www.ancrum.com/activities
  10 Ancrum Road, Lochee, Dundee.

Dundee ScienceMuseum

- Interactive science museum.
  www.dundeesciencecentre.org.uk
  Greenmarket.

Dundee V & A Museum(Free)

- The Dundee branch of London's Victoria and Albert museum, with a focus on design in Scotland.
  www.vam.ac.uk/dundee
  1 Riverside Esplanade.

McManus Gallery andMuseum(Free)

- The Museum is in three sections: tracing Dundee's story, a natural history museum, and an art gallery; plus, exhibitions.
  www.mcmanus.co.uk
  Albert Square, Meadowside.

Mills Observatory (Free)

- Britain's first purpose-built public observatory, come and see the stars and planets. Open in Winter.
  www.leisureandculturedundee.com
  Glamis Road, Balgay Park.

HMS Unicorn

- 46-gun Royal Navy Frigate launched in 1824. One of the six oldest ships in the world and Scotland's only representative from the Royal Navy's days of sail.
  www.frigateunicorn.org
  Victoria Dock.

RRS Discovery

- Built in Dundee and launched in 1901 she was the last traditional wooden three-masted ship to be built in Britain. She earned her place in history as the ship that took Captain Robert Falcon Scott RN and his team to the Antarctic.
  www.rrsdiscovery.co.uk
  Discovery Point, Discovery Quay.

Tay Bridges

- One road bridge opened in 1966, two rail bridges the new one opened in 1887 and the old one opened in 1878 and then collapsed in 1879, killing 75 people. You can still see remnants of it sticking up out of the water.

Verdant Works

- Built in 1833 and turned into a museum in 1996, this was one of many jute factories in Dundee. Many of them still stand, converted into offices and apartments.
  www.verdantworks.co.uk
  West Henderson's Wynd.

North from Dundee

Forfar (Pop. 14,000)

(14 miles North of Dundee)

The town dates back to Roman times. Hungry? Then you should try a "Forfar Bridie" a Scottish meat pastry snack, first made here in town.
There are bus services available, but no trains.
Dundee Airport (16 miles away)
www.hial.co.uk/dundee-airport

- Hotels, B&Bs, Food, Drink, Buses, Taxis, Shops, ATMs/Banks, Medical Center, Museums, **Gas (petrol) & Charging Stations**.

Meffan Museum and Art Gallery

- Find out about local history and the Forfar witches. Also showcasing the work of local, national and internationally renowned artists.
  www.angusalive.scot
  Forfar.

West from Forfar

Restenneth Priory (2 miles West of Forfar)

- The earliest masonry at Restenneth Priory dates to the 1100s. Though much of the church you see today dates from the 1200s. King Alexander 1st of Scotland had the annals of Iona transferred to this site in the 1100s, and King Robert the Bruce buried his young son Prince John here in the 1300s.
  www.historicenvironment.scot
  Forfar.

Glamis Castle (7 miles West of Forfar)

- The ancestral seat to the **Earls of Strathmore and Kinghorne since 1372**, inspiration for Shakespeare's Macbeth, the childhood home of HM Queen Elizabeth the Queen Mother and birthplace of HRH The Princess Margaret.
  www.glamis-castle.co.uk
  Forfar.

Strathmore Highland Games (7 miles West of Forfar)

- Held at Glamis Castle in early-June each year. Tossing the Caber, Highland dancing, Athletics, and Pipe bands.
  www.shottshighlandgames.org.uk
  Glamis Castle, Forfar.

Glenisla Highland Games (20 miles North West of Forfar)

- Held in Late-August each year. Tossing the Caber, Highland dancing, Athletics, and Pipe bands.
  www.glenislahighlandgames.co.uk
  The Haugh, Forfar.

Kirriemuir (Pop. 6,000)

(7 miles North West of Forfar)

Known as the 'Gateway to the Glens' the town dates back to the Iron Age, but the first written record was in 1459 when the burgh of "Kerymure" was created by King James the 2ndof Scotland. The Author of "Peter Pan" J.M. Barrie was born here and there is a "Peter Pan" statue in town to commemorate him. There is also a statue to "Bon Scott" vocalist for the band AC/DC who was born in the hospital in Forfar but raised here. There are bus services available, no trains.
Dundee Airport (24 miles away)
www.hial.co.uk/dundee-airport

- Hotels, B&Bs, Food, Drink, Buses, Taxis, Shops, ATMs/Banks, Medical Center, Museums, **Gas (petrol) & Charging Stations**.

J M Barrie's Birthplace

- The creator of Peter Pan spent his childhood in this small whitewashed cottage. The son of a weaver, Barrie lived with his seven brothers and sisters in two upstairs rooms, while his father's weaving workshop was downstairs. An exhibition tells the story of his life and work.
  www.nts.org.uk
  9 Brechin Road, Kirriemuir.

Kirriemuir Gateway to the Glens Museum
(Free)

- Built as the town's jail and courthouse it has been at the heart of Kirriemuir since its construction in 1604.
  Telling the story of Kirriemuir and the Angus Glens.
  www.angusalive.scot
  32 High Street, Kirriemuir.

Tayside Police Museum (Free)

- Located in the present Police Station. Telling the history of policing in the city of Dundee, and the counties of Perth & Kinross and Angus, from the early 1800s through to the present day.
  http://taysidepolicemuseum.org.uk
  Reform Street, Kirriemuir.

Cortachy Highland Games (5 miles North from Kirrimuir)

- Held in Mid-August each year. Tossing the Caber, Highland dancing, Athletics, and Pipe bands.
  www.cortachygames.co.uk
  Cortachy Castle Grounds, Kirriemuir.

North from Perth

Aberfeldy (Pop. 2,000)

(31 miles North West of Perth)

Aberfeldy came to prominence as a resort town in the 19th century, although the town has been here for far longer, with evidence of fort construction by Roman legions still evident to this day. Nearbyis GlenLyon, widely regarded as one of Scotland's most stunning and least-visited glens. At the mouth of Glen Lyon lies the village of Fortingall, legendary birthplace of Pontius Pilate and home to the Fortingall Yew Tree, reputed to be more than 5,000 years old and one of the oldest trees in the world.
There are buses, but no trains available.
Dundee Airport (50 miles away)
www.hial.co.uk/dundee-airport

- Hotels, B&Bs, Food, Drink, Buses, Shops, ATMs/Banks, Medical Center, **Gas (petrol) & Charging Stations**.

The Birks of Aberfeldy (Free)

- Short, beautiful walk popularized in a song by Robert Burns. Fine walk up the steep gorge of the Moness burn revealing several waterfalls. www.walkhighlands.co.uk
  Moness Burn, Aberfeldy

Aberfeldy Distillery

- Pronunciation: Ab-er-feldy.
- Name Origin: Named after the town of Aberfeldy (Scottish Gaelic - Obar Pheallaidh).
- Established: 1898.
- Location: Near the town of Aberfeldy.
- Region: Highland.
- Visitor Center/Tours: Go to website for information.
- Website:www.dewars.com

Aberfeldy Show and Highland Games

- Held in Early-August each year. Tossing the Caber, Highland dancing, Athletics, and Pipe bands.
  www.aberfeldyshowandgames.co.uk
  Wades Park, Aberfeldy.

Splash White Water Rafting

- As well as White Water Rafting, they do; River Bugging, Paddle Boarding, Duckies, Canyoning, Abseiling and Paintball.
  https://rafting.co.uk
  Dunkeld Road, Aberfeldy.

Side Trip West from Aberfeldy

Castle Menzies (2 miles West from Aberfeldy)

- 16th century castle, the seat of the Chiefs of Clan Menzies for over 500 years. Restored during the twentieth century by the Menzies Clan Society.
  www.castlemenzies.org
  Weem, Aberfeldy.

Kenmore Highland Games (7 miles West from Aberfeldy)

- Held in Early-July each year. Tossing the Caber, Highland dancing, Athletics, and Pipe bands.
  http://www.kenmorehighlandgames.com
  Games Park, Kenmore.

Fortingall Village (8 miles West from Aberfeldy)

- According to legend Pontius Pilate was born here and played in/on the Fortingall Yew tree, reputed to be more than 5,000 years old and one of the oldest trees in the world.
  www.castlemenzies.org
  Weem, Aberfeldy.

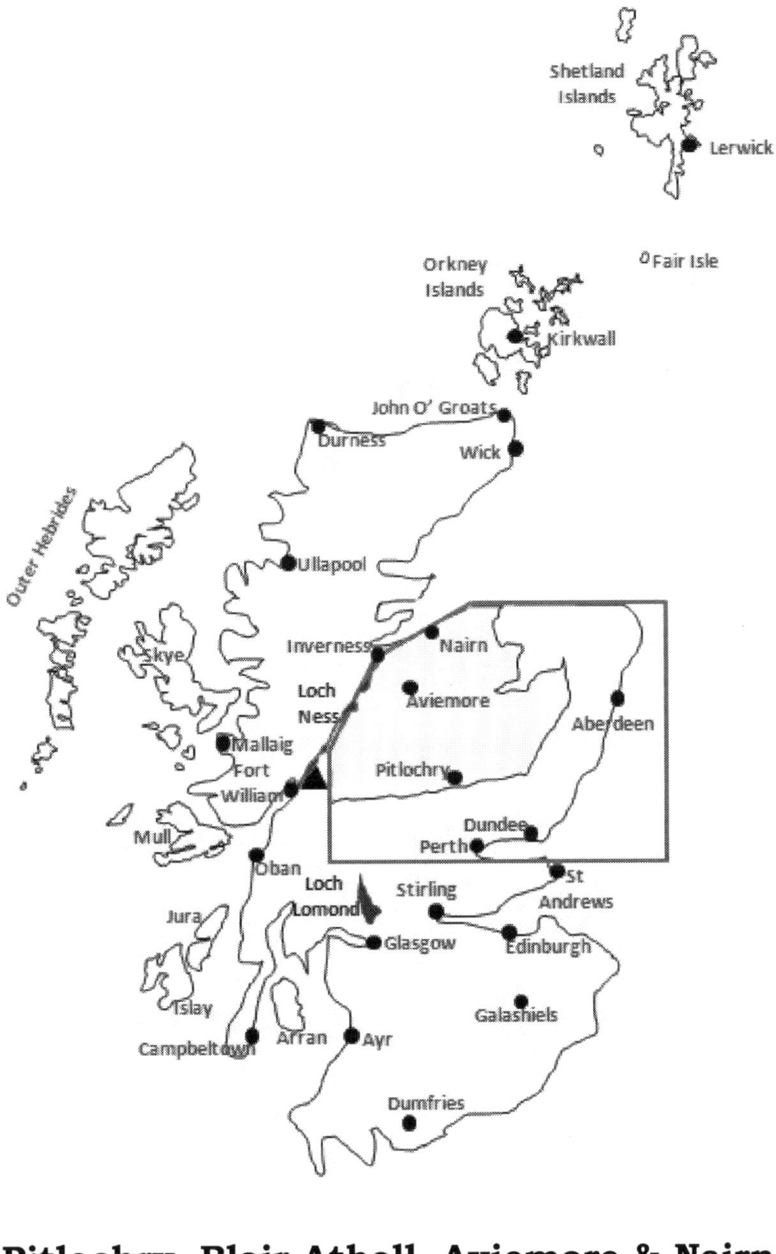

Pitlochry, Blair Atholl, Aviemore & Nairn

In the shaded area shown

The first thing to know about this area is that a large swath of this area is taken up with the "Cairngorms National Park" which encompasses the Cairngorm mountains. After you pass Pitlochry until well past Aviemore everything to your right as you drive North is the park. And to your left is wild mountain country, encompassing Rannoch Moor, 50 square miles of moorland. Yes, there are villages dotted across the landscape and if you stick to the A9 a couple of towns. So, a lot of scenery for you to look at as you drive to your next destination. I have hiked all over this area, and at one point never saw another human for 3 days while walking through the park. Having said that, don't forget Scotland is a small country and you can drive from Pitlochry to Aviemore in just over an hour.

Pitlochry (Pop. 3,000)
(27 miles North of Perth)

Pitlochry was and still is a Victorian town (I'm talking architecture) becoming popular after Queen Victoria bought Balmoral castle and spent many vacations there. The town received a further boost when the railway arrived in1863 and it is still a very popular center for tourists today.
Dundee Airport (49 miles away)
www.hial.co.uk/dundee-airport

- Hotels, B&Bs, Food, Drink, Buses, Taxis, Shops, ATMs/Banks, Hospital, **Gas (petrol) & Charging Stations**.

Atholl Palace Hotel

- Set in 48 acres of gardens/woodland, with swimming pool, Spa, restaurant and whisky bar. We stayed here on our last trip to Scotland, highly recommended.
  www.athollpalace.com
  Perth Road, Pitlochry.

Blair Atholl Distillery

- Pronunciation: Blair Ath-ol.

- Name Origin: Gaelic - "Plain of the new Ireland."

- Established: 1798.

- Location: Pitlochry.

- Region: Highland.

- Visitor Center/Tours: Go to website for information.

- Website:www.malts.com/en-gb/visit-our-distilleries/blair-athol

Pitlochry Highland Games

- Held in Mid-September each year. Tossing the Caber, Highland dancing, Athletics, and Pipe bands.
  www.pitlochryhighlandgames.co.uk
  Ferry Road, Pitlochry.

Edradour Distillery

- Pronunciation: Ed-rad-hour
- Name Origin: Gaelic - "Between two waters."
- Established: 1937.
- Location: Pitlochry.
- Region: Highland.
- Visitor Center/Tours: Go to website for information.
- Website: https

North from Pitlochry

Killiecrankie visitor center(4 miles North from Pitlochry)

- Site of the 27th July 1689 battle (one of Scotland's bloodiest) between the Jacobites and the British Redcoats in a beautiful wooded gorge. While here make sure to see the "soldier's leap," where a fleeing Redcoat soldiers leapt 18 feet across the river Garry to escape his Jacobite pursuers.
  www.nts.org.uk
  Killiecrankie, Pitlochry.

East from

Strathardle Highland Games (12 miles East from Pitlochry)

- Held in Late-August each year. Tossing the Caber, Highland dancing, Athletics, and Pipe bands.
  https://strathardlehighlandgathering.org.uk
  Bannerfield, Strathardle.

N

W E

S

West from

Fonab Castle Hotel(2 miles West from Pitlochry)

- The hotel offers a choice of two restaurants and a cellar with a fine selection of wines, whiskies and gins.
  www.fonabcastlehotel.com
  Foss Road, Pitlochry.

Queen's View Visitor Center(7 miles West from Pitlochry)

- When Queen Victoria visited in 1866, she assumed that the sweeping view west along Loch Tummel was named after her, but it is more likely named for Queen Isabella, the first wife of King Robert the Bruce.
  https://forestryandland.gov.scot
  Pitlochry.

Rannoch Highland Games (21 miles West from Pitlochry)

- Held in Late-August each year. Tossing the Caber, Highland dancing, Athletics, and Pipe bands.
  www.rannochhighlandgathering.co.uk
  Kinloch Rannoch, Pitlochry.

Blair Atholl (Pop. 600)

(7 miles North from Pitlochry)

Blair Atholl is a modern village by Scottish standards being around 100 years old. The main route North/South is the A9 which passes close by the village, and there are two things that will catch your eye as you approach; Blair Castle and the "House of Bruar," more details on both below.
Bus and Train services available.
Dundee Airport (57 miles away)
www.hial.co.uk/dundee-airport

- Hotels, B&Bs, Food, Drink, Buses, Taxis, Shops, ATMand **Charging Stations**.

The Atholl Gathering and Highland Games

- Europe's last remaining private army, the Atholl Highlanders officially open the Highland Games with a 'March On', led by their pipes and drums. All the usual Highland games events. Held each year in late May.
  https://blair-castle.co.uk
  Blair Atholl, *Pitlochry.*

Blair Castle

- The Castle is believed to have been started in 1269 by John Comyn, Lord of Baneoch. In 1629 John Murray, son of the second Earl of Tullibardine, was created Earl of Atholl, the title and castle have remained in the Murray family ever since. In 1702 Queen Anne created the first Duke ofAtholl. The castle is also famous for Europe's last remaining private army, the Atholl Highlanders.
  https://blair-castle.co.uk
  Blair Athol, Pitlochry.

North from Blair Atholl

House of Bruar(4 miles North from Blair Atholl)

- The UK's Leading Scottish Country Clothing Specialist, with a food hall full of top-quality Scottish food and Drink. There is also a gallery selling Scottish art and a café. I'm not someone that generally likes to shop, but I am always glad to stop here.
  https://forestryandland.gov.scot
  Pitlochry.

Dalwhinnie Distillery(24 miles North fromBlair Atholl)

- Pronunciation: Dal-whin-ae
- Name Origin: Gaelic – “Field of the champion."
- Established: 1897.
- Location: General Wade's Military Road, Dalwhinnie.
- Region: Highland.
- Visitor Center/Tours: Go to website for information.
- Website:www.malts.com/en-us/distilleries/dalwhinnie

Glentruim Castle & Cottages(32 miles North from Blair Atholl)

- The castle was built as a family home in the early 1840’s by Major Euan Macpherson. Self-catering holiday and luxury accommodation (meals can be booked in advance, if you do not wish to cook) surrounded by the Cairngorm National Park. www.glentruimestate.co.uk
  Glentruim Estate, Newtonmore.

Newtonmore Highland Games (34 miles North from Blair Atholl)

- Held in Early-August each year. Tossing the Caber, Highland dancing, Athletics, and Pipe bands.
  www.newtonmorehighlandgames.co.uk
  The Eilan, Newtonmore

Highland Folk Museum(35 miles North from Blair Atholl)

- 80 acre living history site. Visitors can discover how Highland people lived, worked and dressed, how they produced food, cooked and what they ate from the 1700s up to 1950s.
  www.highlifehighland.com
  Aultlarie Croft, Kingussie Road, Newtonmore.

Ruthven Barracks(39 miles North from Blair Atholl)

- Built by the British government between 1719 and 1721 following the Jacobite rising of 1715. They were to house two companies of soldiers, about 120 men to control the area.
  www.historicenvironment.scot
  Kingussie.

ArdverikieCastle Estate (40 miles North from Blair Atholl)

- Victorian Gothic castle, used in the filming of "Monarch of the Glen" TV series as "Glen Bogle." Although you cannot stay in the castle itself, they have holiday cottages available and you can stay in the gatehouse.
  www.ardverikie.com
  Kinloch Laggan, Newtonmore.

Speyside Distillery(40 miles North from Blair Atholl)

- Pronunciation: Spey-Side.
- Name Origin: Gaelic - "Thorn side."
- Established: 1990.
- Location: Tromie Mills, Kingussie.
- Region: Speyside.
- Visitor Center/Tours: Go to website for information.
- Website: https

G2 Outdoor (45 miles North from Blair Atholl)

- For outdoor activities such as white-water rafting, canyoning, mountain biking or gorge walking.
  www.g2outdoor.co.uk
  The Hatchery, Alvie Estate, Aviemore.

Zip Trek Adventure Park Aviemore (47 miles North from Blair Atholl)

- Two separate courses that allow you to fly through the trees on a Scottish estate in the Cairngorm mountains.
  www.zippark.co.uk
  Delfour Hatchery, Alvie Estate, Aviemore.

Aviemore (Pop. 2,500)

(51 miles NorthWestfromBlair Atholl)

Aviemore was an isolated outpost in the highlands until the railway arrived in 1862. Although Aviemore was now accessible it took until the early 1960s for the town to really get on the map when the UKs first ski resort was opened here. The emphasis here is on outdoor pursuits, but there is also a theatre, a swimming pool, a go-carting track. Good bus and train services.
InvernessAirport (36 miles away)
www.invernessairport.co.uk

- Hotels, B&Bs, Food, Drink, Buses, Taxis, Shops, ATMs/Bank, Medical Center, **Gas (petrol) & Charging Stations**.

Strathspey Steam Railway

- Take a trip on a steam train through beautiful scenery. Dinners and Sunday lunch trips can be booked.
  www.cairngormreindeer.co.uk
  Aviemore.

Thunder in the Glens

- This motorcycle rally attracts over 10,000 visitors to Aviemore and the Speyside areas on the last weekend in August.
  www.titg.co.uk
  Aviemore.

Side trip East from Aviemore

Cairngorm Reindeer Center (9 miles East from Aviemore)

- The UKs only free-ranging reindeer herd (around 150) the Shop and Paddocks are open daily (except Jan-early Feb) and there is a daily guided Hill Trip to see the tame and friendly reindeer.
  www.cairngormreindeer.co.uk
  Aviemore.

North from Aviemore

Landmark Forest Adventure Park (7 miles North from Aviemore)

- Family Adventure Park; Ant City, Bamboozeleum, Dinosaur Kingdom, Forest Safari Ride, Forest Trail, Lost Labyrinth, Mini Diggers, Nature Trail, Ropeworx, Runaway Timber Train, Shooting Gallery, Tarzan Trail, Tropical Hothouse, Wee Monkey Trail, Wild Water Coaster, Wonderwood. www.landmarkpark.co.uk

  Carrbridge.

Kenmore Highland Games (12 miles North from Aviemore)

- Held in Early-August each year. Tossing the Caber, Highland dancing, Athletics, and Pipe bands.
  https://nethybridge.com/abernethy-highland-games
  Games Field, Nethy Bridge.

Tomatin Distillery (16 miles North from Aviemore)

- Pronunciation: Tom-a-Tin.
- Name Origin: Gaelic - "Juniper hill."
- Established: 1897.
- Location: Tomatin.
- Region: Highland.
- Visitor Center/Tours: Go to website for information.
- Website:www.tomatin.com

Culloden Battlefield (29 miles North from Aviemore and 8 miles from Inverness)

- The last battle to be fought on British soil, took place on 16th April 1746 Culloden, just outside the town of Inverness. Where British government forces defeated Bonnie Prince Charlie's Jacobite army. www.nts.org.uk/visit/places/culloden *Culloden Moor, Inverness.*

Clava Cairns(31 miles North from Aviemore and 7 miles from Inverness)

- Ancient Burial grounds, dating back around 4,000 years. www.visitinvernesslochness.com/property/clava-cairns-inverness *Inverness.*

Fort George(40 miles North from Aviemore and 13 miles from Inverness)

- 18th-century fortified garrison and working army barracks, housing Highlanders regimental museum. Taking 22 years to complete, one of Europe's most outstanding forts.
  www.historicenvironment.scot
  Near, Ardersier, Inverness.

Cawdor Castle(40 miles North from Aviemore and 14 miles from Inverness)

- Dating from the late 14th century and home to the Earl of Cawdor.
  www.cawdorcastle.com
  Cawdor, Nairn.

Nairn (Pop. 10,000)

(33 miles North from Aviemore and 16 miles from Inverness)

Nairn can trace its history back to the Bronze age, but now is best known as a seaside resort and for its two golf courses. Bus and train services available. InvernessAirport (9 miles away)
www.invernessairport.co.uk

- Hotels, B&Bs, Food, Drink, Buses, Taxis, Shops, ATMs/Bank, Hospital, **Gas (petrol) & Charging Stations**.

Nairn Highland Games

- Held in Late-August each year. Tossing the Caber, Highland dancing, Athletics, and Pipe bands.
  http://nairnhighlandgames.co.uk
  Nairn Central Links, Nairn.

Brodie Castle(7 miles East from Nairn)

- Ancestral home of the Brodie clan for over 400 years. The castle houses a magnificent collection of furniture, ceramics and artwork, including works by 17th-century Dutch masters and 20th-century Scottish Colorists. It also boasts an impressive library containing over 6,000 volumes.
  www.nts.org.uk/visit/places/brodie-castle
  Brodie, Forres.

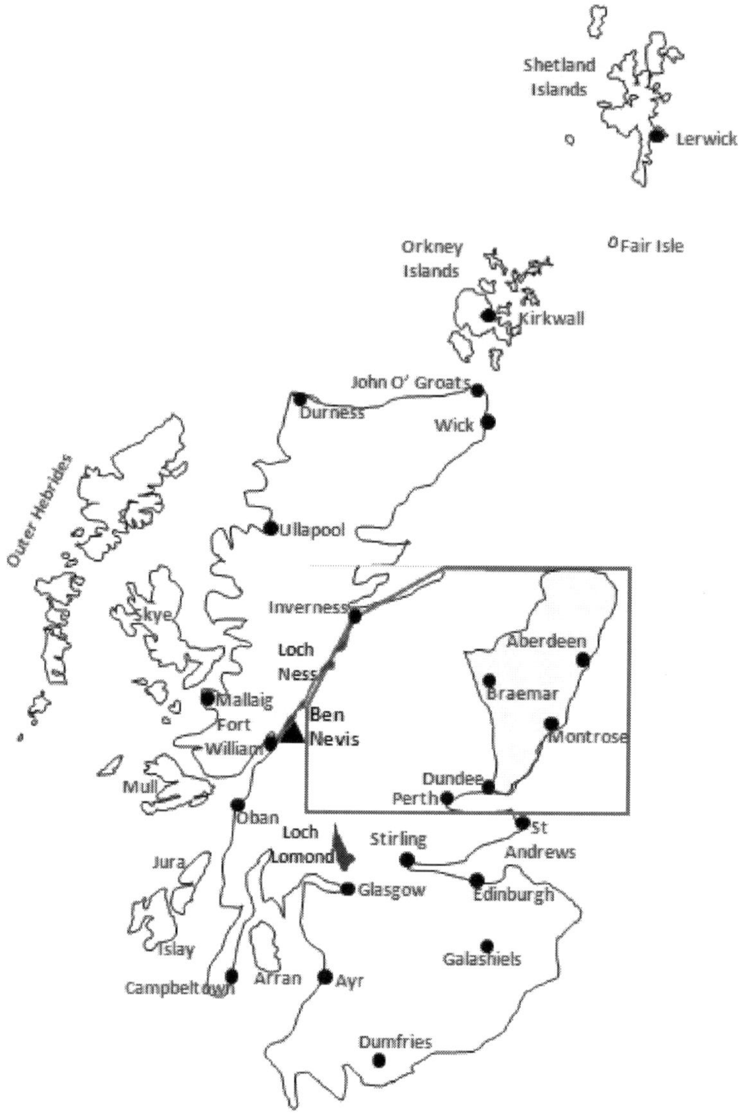

Arbroath, Montrose, Stonehaven, AberdeenandPeterhead

In the shaded area shown.

North from Dundee

Arbroath (Pop. 24,000)

(17 miles North East of Dundee)

The town was first mentioned in written history with the founding of Arbroath Abbey in 1178. This is the town where the "Declaration of Arbroath" was written in 1320 with the now famous line;

"For, as long as but a hundred of us remain alive, never will we on any conditions be brought under English rule. It is in truth not for glory, nor riches, nor honours that we are fighting, but for freedom – for that alone, which no honest man gives up but with life itself."

Hungry? Then you should try an "Arbroath Smokie" a Haddock smoked over wood chips, first made here in town.
There are bus and train services available.
Dundee Airport (19 miles away)
www.hial.co.uk/dundee-airport

- Hotels, B&Bs, Food, Drink, Car Hire, Buses, Taxis, Shops, ATMs/Banks, Hospital, Museums, **Gas (petrol) & Charging Stations**.

Arbroath Abbey (Free)

- Founded in 1178 by King William the Lion, the abbey was one of the nation's grandest monasteries for almost 400 years.
  www.historicenvironment.scot
  Abbey Street, Arbroath.

Arbroath Signal Tower Museum (Free)

- The museum tells the story of Arbroath's fishing and maritime industries.
  www.angusalive.scot
  Ladyloan, Arbroath.

Declaration of Arbroath Monument (Free)

- Statue commemorating the "Declaration of Arbroath."
  1QD, Dundee Road, Arbroath.

Keptie Water Tower(Free)

- Water Tower disguised as a small castle, overlooking Keptie pond.
  36 Hillend Road, Arbroath.

North from Arbroath

Dunninald Castle(11 miles North of Arbroath)

- The present castle was built in 1824 in the Gothic Revival style. This was the 3rd castle built, the first being built around 1000 years ago and the second around 1590.
  www.dunninald.com
  Dunninald Castle, Montrose.

Montrose (Pop. 12,000)

(13 miles North of Arbroath)

The town was granted a Royal Charter by King David the 1st in the 1100s, although the town was there for a long time prior to this.
There are bus and train services available.
Dundee Airport (32 miles away)
www.hial.co.uk/dundee-airport

- Hotels, B&Bs, Food, Drink, Car Hire, Buses, Taxis, Shops, ATMs/Banks, Medical Center, Museums, **Gas (petrol) & Charging Stations**.

Montrose Museum (Free)

- Telling the story of Montrose and its people, from the earliest archaeological finds to the Marquis of Montrose and the Jacobite uprisings, the harbour and maritime trade.
  www.angusalive.scot
  Panmure Place, Montrose.

Montrose Air Station Heritage Centre

- Telling the story of the airfield, the men and women who served there and also the local people. This was the first operational airfield in Britain, established by the Royal Flying Corps in 1913.
  https://rafmontrose.org.uk
  Waldron Road, Montrose.

Fettercairn Distillery(13 miles North of Montrose)

- Pronunciation: Fet-er-cairn
- Name Origin: Gaelic - "The foot of the mountain"
- Established: 1824.
- Location: Distillery Road, Fettercairn Laurencekirk.
- Region: Highland.
- Visitor Center/Tours: Go to website for information.
- Website:www.fettercairnwhisky.com

Dunnotter Castle(21 miles North of Montrose)

- Perched atop a 440 million-year-old rock makes this castle a formidable stronghold and not easily taken by force. Oliver Cromwell's army laid siege to Dunnottar and its small garrison for eight months and failed to take it. Mary Queen of Scots, the Marquis of Montrose, William Wallace, and the future King Charles have all stayed here.
  www.dunnottarcastle.co.uk
  Stonehaven.

Side Trip West from Montrose

Glencadam Distillery(8 miles West of Montrose)

- Pronunciation: Glen-cad-am.
- Name Origin: Gaelic - "Valley slope."
- Established: 1825.
- Location: Brechin, Angus.
- Region: Highland.
- Visitor Center/Tours: Go to website for information.
- Website:www.glencadamwhisky.com

North from Montrose

Stonehaven (Pop. 12,000)

(23 miles North East of Montrose)

Stonehaven started life as an Iron-age fishing village and the main focus of the town is still its harbor.
There are bus and train services available.
Aberdeen Airport (Dyce) (18 miles away)
www.aberdeenairport.com

- Hotels, B&Bs, Food, Drink, Buses, Taxis, Shops, ATMs/Banks, Hospital, **Gas (petrol) & Charging Stations**.

Stonehaven Fire Festival

- The town has a very different way of welcoming in the new year. As the bells ring in the new year at midnight on December 31st around 40 men and women parade up and down the main street swinging flaming fireballs around their heads.
  http://stonehavenfireballs.co.uk
  Stonehaven.

Stonehaven Folk Festival

- Over 50 events from on stage performances to informal performances in pubs and around the harbor. Held each year in mid-July.
  www.stonehavenfolkfestival.co.uk
  Stonehaven

Stonehaven Highland Games

- All the standard games events including; Highland Dancing, piping competitions, Running Events, Throwing the Hammer, Tossing the Caber and Tug o' War.
  Held each year in late July.
  http://stonehavenhighlandgames.com
  Stonehaven.

Ardoe House (13 miles North from Stonehaven)

- 19th-century mansion house set in 30 acres.
  https://all.accor.com/hotel/6626/index.en.shtml
  Aberdeen.

Drumtochty Highland Games(13 miles West from Stonehaven)

- Held at the castle in Late-June each year. Tossing the Caber, Highland dancing, Athletics, and Pipe bands.
  www.spanglefish.com/drumtochtyhighlandgames
  Laurencekirk.

Aboyne Highland Games (28 miles West of Stonehaven)

- Held in Early-August each year. Tossing the Caber, Highland dancing, Athletics, and Pipe bands.
  www.aboynegames.com
  Village Green, Aboyne.

Ballater Highland Games (38 miles West of Stonehaven)

- Held in Early-August each year. Tossing the Caber, Highland dancing, Athletics, and Pipe bands.
  www.ballaterhighlandgaUnapoolmes.com
  Monaltrie Park, Provost Craig Road, Ballater.

North from Stonehaven

Aberdeen (Pop. 197,000)

(16 miles North of Stonehaven)

Aberdeen is Scotland's third largest city and is known as the "Granite city" as most of its buildings are built out of granite. These give Aberdeen one of the most celebrated cityscapes in Britain.
There has been a settlement here for around 8,000 years. Aberdeen has 3 cathedrals and a University established in 1495. The local Scots dialect is called Doric and differs from the standard Scots and can be a little confusing to hear, but you will soon realize what it is being said to you.
Aberdeen is known as the European oil CapitaLand its harbor is busy with shipping related to the North Sea Oil industry.
There are good bus and train services available.
Aberdeen Airport (Dyce) (6 miles from Aberdeen)
www.aberdeenairport.com
Ferries to the Orkney and Shetland islands.
www.northlinkferries.co.uk/ports/aberdeen

- Hotels, B&Bs, Food, Drink, Buses, Taxis, Shops, ATMs/Banks, Museums, Hospital, **Gas (petrol) & Charging Stations**.

Aberdeen Art Gallery (Free)

- Hosting many modern and traditional art pieces.
  www.aagm.co.uk
  Schoolhill, Aberdeen.

Aberdeen Distillery and Gin School

- The distillery is open to visitors, for tastings, tours, masterclass and a school where you can distill your own gin.
  https://cityofaberdeendistillery.co.uk
  Arch 10 Palmerston Road, Aberdeen.

Aberdeen Highland Games

- Including traditional Scottish Highland Games competitions, pipe band championships and solo piping competitions, as well as a funfair, family entertainment stage performances, free children's activities, catering outlets and a beer tent.
  www.aberdeencity.gov.uk
  Hazlehead Avenue, Aberdeen.

Aberdeen Jazz Festival

- Showcasing live jazz performances with musicians from around the world, held at several different venues. Held in March each year.
  www.aberdeenjazzfestival.com
  Various venues, Aberdeen.

Aberdeen Maritime Museum(Free)

- Telling the city's long relationship with the sea.
  www.aagm.co.uk
  Shiprow, Aberdeen.

Aberdeen May Festival

- Featuring films, food, Gaelic, literature, music, science and sport. Held in late May each year.
  www.abdn.ac.uk/mayfestival
  Various venues, Aberdeen.

Aberdeen Science Centre

- Housed in what was the main depot for the city's tram system. With over 50 hands on exhibits.
  www.aberdeensciencecentre.org
  107 George Street, Aberdeen.

Kings Museum (Free)

- At the University of Aberdeen's King's College campus, while here you can also visit the University library on the 7th floor offering great views over the harbor and city (also Free).
  www.abdn.ac.uk
  Town House, University of Aberdeen, High Street, Aberdeen.

Provost Skene's House (Free)

- Scottish towns and cities have a "provost" instead of a mayor and this house as the name suggests used to belong to Provost George Skene. Dating from 1545, this large, house is the oldest in the city. Housing rooms showcasing furniture from the 17th, 18th and 19th century.
  www.aagm.co.uk
  Guestrow, Flourmill Lane, Aberdeen.

St. Andrew's Cathedral(Not 'THE' St Andrew's cathedral)

- Early-1800s Episcopal church built of sandstone & granite.
  www.standrewscathedralaberdeen.org.uk
  28 King Street, Aberdeen.

St. Mary's Cathedral

- Catholic Cathedral opened in 1860.
  www.rcda.scot
  16-20 Huntly Street, Aberdeen.

St. Machar's Cathedral

- Church of Scotland Cathedral opened in 1530, although it is believed a place of worship was established on this location in the year 580.
  www.stmachar.com
  The Chanonry, Old Aberdeen, Aberdeen.

The Gordon Highlanders Museum

- Tells the story of one of the British Army's most famous regiments, with its soldiers mainly recruited from the local area in the North East of Scotland.
  https://gordonhighlanders.com
  St. Luke's, Viewfield Road, Aberdeen.

Tolbooth Museum (Free)

- Housed in a 17th century Tolbooth (Town Hall, providing council meeting space, a courthouse and jail), this is Aberdeen's museum of civic history. Included in the displays is the blade from Aberdeen's 17th century Guillotine.
  www.aagm.co.uk
  Castle Street, Aberdeen.

Zoology Museum (Free)

- At the University of Aberdeen's King's College campus, Exhibits include taxidermy, skeletons, skins, fluid-preserved specimens and models.
  www.abdn.ac.uk
  Tillydrone Avenue, Aberdeen.

Side Trip West from Aberdeen

Drum Castle (12 miles West of Aberdeen)

- The tower of Drum and the surrounding Royal forest were given to the Irvine family 1323 by King Robert the Bruce of Scotland. The family subsequently added a Jacobean mansion.
  www.nts.org.uk
  Drumoak, Banchory.

Royal Deeside Railway (18 miles West of Aberdeen City Center)

- Steam and Diesel heritage railway offering trips on the one-mile line along the River Dee. Victorian train station, tea-room, art gallery, and craft shops.
  www.nts.org.uk
  Milton of Crathes, Banchory.

Craigievar Castle (27 miles West of Aberdeen City Center)

- Scotland's beautiful pink castle built in the Scottish Baronial style and completed 1626. www.historicenvironment.scot *Craigievar, Alford.*

Ardmore Distillery(36 miles West of Aberdeen City Center)

- Pronunciation: Ard-more.
- Name Origin: Gaelic - "Big height."
- Established: 1898.
- Location: Kennethmont, Aberdeenshire.
- Region: Highland.
- Visitor Center/Tours: Go to website for information.
- Website:www.ardmorewhisky.com

Kildrummy Castle (36 miles West of Aberdeen City Center)

- The castle may be a ruin now, but it's an impressive one, built in the 13th century for the Earls of Mar.
  www.historicenvironment.scot
  Kildrummy, Alford.

Lonach Highland Gathering & Games
(42 miles West from Aberdeen)

- Held on the 4th Saturday of August each year. Tossing the Caber, Highland dancing, Athletics, and Pipe bands.
  www.lonach.org
  Bellabeg Park, Strathdon.

Bamoral Castle (47 miles West of Aberdeen City Center)

- Balmoral has belonged to the British Royal Family since 1852, when the estate and its original castle were bought from the Farquason family by Prince Albert (who commissioned the current castle to be built), the husband of Queen Victoria.
  www.balmoralcastle.com
  Balmoral Estates, Ballater.

Royal lochnagar Distillery (48 miles West of Aberdeen City Center)

- Pronunciation: Royal Loch-Na-Garr
- Name Origin: Gaelic - "Loch of noise/laughter."
- Established: 1845.
- Location: Easter Balmoral, Ballater.
- Region: Highland.
- Visitor Center/Tours: Go to website for information.
- Website:www.malts.com/en-row/distilleries/royal-lochnagar/tours

Crathie Kirk (47 miles West of Aberdeen City Center)

- The present church dates from 1895, though there were many on this site prior to this. It was to this church that Queen Victoria came in 1848 on coming to Balmoral Castle. This began the custom, which continues to this day, of members of the Royal Family and their guests worshipping with local people in the parish church.
  http://braemarandcrathieparish.org.uk
  2 Fergach Cottages, Crathie, Ballater.

Corgarff Castle (50 miles West of Aberdeen City Center)

- Built in the mid-1500s with a unique star shaped design around its base.
  www.historicenvironment.scot
  8m W of Strathdon on the, A939, Strathdon.

Braemar (Pop. 1,000)

(56 miles West of Aberdeen)

According to legend, King Malcolm the 3rd of Scotland came here around 1059 and built a timber bridge over the Clunie water.
I have not stayed in any hotels here I did however spend the night at the youth hostel while hiking solo across Scotland a few years ago and can recommend it if you are considering youth hostels.
There are buses, but the nearest train station is in Pitlochry 45 miles away.
Aberdeen Airport (Dyce) (54 miles away)
www.aberdeenairport.com

- Hotels, B&Bs, Food, Drink, Buses, Shops, ATMs, Medical center, **Gas (petrol) & Charging Station**.

Braemar Gathering

- Annual Highland games held in Braemar on the first Saturday in September and traditionally attended by the British Royal Family.
  www.braemargathering.org
  Princess Royal and Duke of Fife Memorial Park, Braemar.

Braemar Junior Highland Games

- Junior Highland games held in Braemar in Mid-July. Tossing the Caber, Highland dancing, Athletics, and Pipe bands.
  www.braemarjuniorgames.com
  Princess Royal and Duke of Fife Memorial Park, Braemar.

Braemar Castle

- The present Castle was constructed in 1628 by John Erskine, Earl of Mar, as a hunting lodge.
  www.braemarcastle.co.uk
  Braemar, Ballater.

Fife Arms Hotel

- Victorian coaching inn built in the 19th century.
  https://thefifearms.com
  Mar Road, Braemar, Ballater.

North from Aberdeen

Macleod House and Lodge (11 miles North from Aberdeen City Center)

- Historic mansion house which has been extensively renovated to make it into a 19-bedroom luxury hotel.
  www.trumphotels.com
  Aberdeen.

Glen Garioch Distillery(18 miles North from Aberdeen City Center)

- Pronunciation: Glen-Geery.
- Name Origin: Gaelic - "Glen of the Rough ground."
- Established: 1797.
- Location: Inverurie, Oldmeldrum, Distillery Road.
- Region: Highland.
- Visitor Center/Tours: Go to website for information.
- Website:www.glengarioch.com

Old Meldrum Sports and Highland Games
(18 miles North from Aberdeen)

- Held in Mid-June each year. Tossing the Caber, Highland dancing, Athletics, and Pipe bands.
  www.oldmeldrumsports.co.uk
  Park Cresent, Oldmeldrum, Inverurie.

Haddo House and Estate(20 miles North from Aberdeen City Center)

- Built in 1732 and home to the Gordon family for over 400 years. Combining Georgian architecture with sumptuous Victorian interiors.
  http://visithaddo.com
  Methlick, Ellon.

Leslie Castle Hotel(29 miles North from Aberdeen City Center)

- Built in 1661, Leslie Castle now offers delightful adults only, B&B. Delicious Scottish breakfasts are cooked to order, dinner can be provided if you book in advance.
  https://leslie-castle.com
  Leslie, Insch.

Peterhead (Pop. 19,000)

(32 miles North of Aberdeen)

Peterhead was and is a fishing town and it's first harbor was built in 1593. The large harbor is also used in support of the North Sea Oil industry.
There are buses, but no trains, the nearest train station is Aberdeen.
Aberdeen Airport (Dyce)(36 miles away)
www.aberdeenairport.com

- Hotels, B&Bs, Food, Drink, Buses, Taxis, Shops, ATMs/Banks, Hospital, **Gas (petrol) & Charging Stations**.

Peterhead Prison Museum

- Built in the Victorian era, the Prison is unique in that it had the first state owned railway in the UK and saw the only time the SAS (Special Air Service) were used to end a domestic siege in mainland Britain.
  https://peterheadprisonmuseum.com
  South Road, Peterhead.

North from Peterhead

Maggie's Hoosie (16 miles North of Peterhead)

- Local cottage representing the life of the fisherwoman who lived there. With earthen floors, no electricity or running water where she baited fishing lines, cured, smoked, salted and dried fish.
  http://discoverfraserburgh.com
  Fraserburgh.

Kinnaird Head Castle Lighthouse Museum (18 miles North of Peterhead)

- The castle was built in the 1500s and turned into a lighthouse in 1786. The building is completely intact making for a unique museum.
  www.historicenvironment.scot
  Fraserburgh.

Side Trip West from Peterhead

Duff House(35 miles West of Peterhead)

- 18th century stately home of William Duff Lord Braco, later the 1st Earl of Fife.
  www.historicenvironment.scot
  Banff.

Glen Deveron Distillery(MacDuff) (35 miles West of Peterhead)

- Pronunciation: Glen-def-er-on.
- Name Origin: Gaelic - "Glen of the black earn."
- Established: 1962.
- Location: Banff, Aberdeenshire.
- Region: Speyside.
- Visitor Center/Tours: No tours.
- Website: https

Glendronach Distillery (37 miles West of Peterhead)

- Pronunciation: Glen-Dron-Ak.
- Name Origin: Gaelic - "Valley of the Blackberries."
- Established: 1826.
- Location: Forgue by Huntly.
- Region: Highland.
- Visitor Center/Tours: Go to website for information.
- Website:www.glendronachdistillery.com

Cornhill Highland Games (43 miles West from Peterhead)

- Held early-June each year. Tossing the Caber, Highland dancing, Athletics, and Pipe bands. www.shottshighlandgames.org.uk
  Cornhill Playing Field, Banff.

Scottish Traditional Boat Festival
(43 West of Peterhead)

- With boats (competitive sailing), music, crafts, food and drinkheld annually in late-June in Portsoy.
  www.stbfportsoy.org

Huntly Castle (48 miles West of Peterhead)

- Built in the late 12th century for the Earls of Fife, latterly becoming the seat of the Earls of Huntly one of medieval Scotland's most powerful families. Heraldic sculpture and inscribed stone friezes.
  www.historicenvironment.scot
  Huntly.

Knochdhu Distillery(48 miles West of Peterhead)

- Pronunciation: Nock-doo.
- Name Origin: Gaelic - "Little black hill."
- Established: 1894
- Location: Knock, Huntly Aberdeenshire.
- Region: Highland.
- Visitor Center/Tours: Go to website for information.
- Website: https

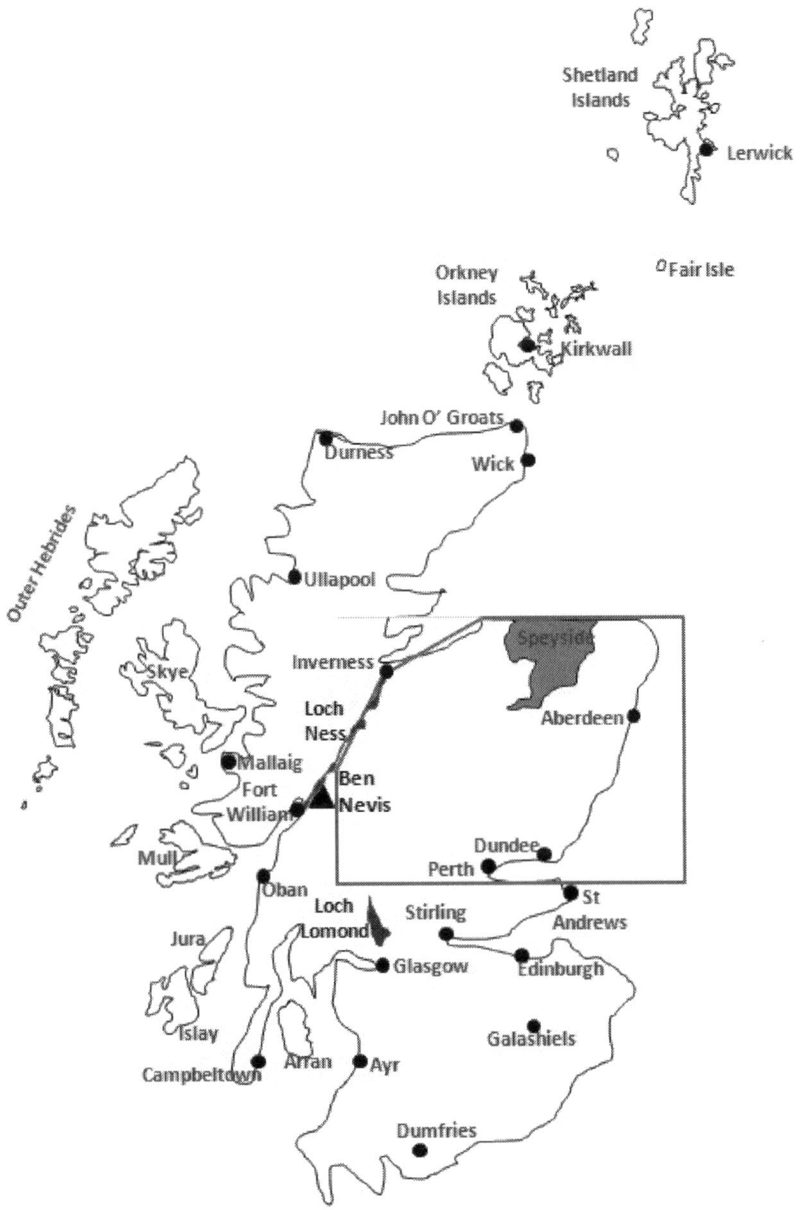

Speyside the heart of whisky distilling

In the shaded area shown.

Spirit of Speyside Whisky Festival

- Various locations throughout Moray Speysideincluding many famous distilleries. Held late April, early May each year. www.spiritofspeyside.com

Spirit of Speyside Distilled: Food & Drink

- Various locations throughout Moray Speyside. Held Early September each year. www.spiritofspeyside.com

Spirit of the North Festival

- Various locations throughout Moray Speyside. Held Late-September each year. www.spiritofspeyside.com

Elgin(Pop. 23,000)

(38 miles East from Inverness and 66 miles West from Aberdeen)

The city of Elgin was first documented in the Cartulary of Moray in 1190 AD and is best known for its ruined cathedral destroyed by Alexander Stewart, Earl of Buchan known as the "Wolf of Badenoch." I will be using Elgin as the anchor point for all sites in the Speyside area.
Good bus and train services available.
Inverness Airport(32 miles away)
www.invernessairport.co.uk

- Hotels, B&Bs, Food, Drink, Buses, Taxis, Shops, ATMs/Banks, Museums, Hospital, **Gas (petrol) & Charging Stations**.

The Lodge Guesthouse

- We stayed here (for Bed & Breakfast) when we were in Elgin. The lodge was built for a tea-planter returning home to retire and is set in a large mature garden.
  www.thelodge-elgin.com
  20 Duff Avenue, Elgin.

Elgin Cathedral

- Known as the 'Lantern of the North' the cathedral was started in 1224. Although it is now a ruin, it is still an amazing site.
  www.historicenvironment.scot
  King Street, Elgin.

Elgin Museum

- Here you can see objects from all over the world, with a special focus on Moray, and from all periods of history and prehistory – from before the dinosaurs to the present day.
  https://elginmuseum.org.uk
  1 High Street, Elgin.

Glen Moray Distillery

- Pronunciation: Glen-Mor-ray
- Name Origin: Gaelic - "Valley, sea settlement."
- Established: 1897.
- Location: Bruceland road, Elgin.
- Region: Speyside.
- Visitor Center/Tours: Go to website for information.
- Website:www.glenmoray.com

Linkwood Distillery

- Pronunciation: Link-wood.
- Name Origin: From the road, the distillery is built on.
- Established: 1821.
- Location: Linkwood Road, Elgin.
- Region: Speyside.
- Visitor Center/Tours: Go to website for information.
- Website:www.malts.com/en-us/our-whisky-collection/linkwood

Moray Motor Museum

- With a superb collection of vintage and classic cars and motorbikes.
  https://moraymotormuseum.org
  Bridge Street, Elgin.

N

W E

S

North from Elgin

Spynie Palace(3 miles North from Elgin)

- The largest surviving medieval bishop's house in Scotland – residence of the bishops of Moray for 500 years.
  www.historicenvironment.scot
  Near, Elgin.

Dufus Castle(5 miles North from Elgin)

- This castle was home to the Moray family for over 500 years, from the 1100s to the 1700s. The stone castle we see today was built in the 1300s, replacing an earlier timber fortress.
  www.historicenvironment.scot
  Near, Elgin.

Covesea Lighthouse, Royal Navy and Royal Air Force Heritage Centre

(7 miles North from Elgin)

- Completed in 1846, the Lighthouse is situated on the outskirts of Lossiemouth on the Moray Firth Coast (voted one of the most breathtaking coasts in the world in a National Geographic Traveler magazine survey).
  http://covesealighthouse.co.uk
  Covesea, Lossiemouth.

South from Elgin

Benriach Distillery (4 miles South from Elgin)

- Pronunciation: Ben-Ree-Ak
- Name Origin: Gaelic - "Speckled Mountain."
- Established: 1898.
- Location: Elgin.
- Region: Speyside.
- Visitor Center/Tours: Go to website for information.
- Website:www.benriachdistillery.com

Glen Grant Distillery(10 miles South from Elgin)

- Pronunciation: Glen-Grant
- Name Origin: Gaelic - "Grant's valley."
- Established: 1840.
- Location: Elgin Road, Rothes.
- Region: Speyside.
- Visitor Center/Tours: Go to website for information.
- Website:www.glengrant.com

Speyburn Distillery (10 miles South from Elgin)

- Pronunciation: Spey-Burn
- Name Origin: Gaelic - "Thorn burn."
- Established: 1897.
- Location: Rothes, Aberlour.
- Region: Speyside.
- Visitor Center/Tours: Go to website for information.
- Website:www.speyburn.com

Glenrothes Distillery (11 miles South from Elgin)

- Pronunciation: Glen-Roth-is.
- Name Origin: Gaelic - "Valley of the 'Rothes,' the family who owned the land.
- Established: 1878.
- Location: Rothes.
- Region: Speyside.
- Visitor Center/Tours: Go to website for information.
- Website:www.theglenrothes.com

Craigellachie Distillery (14 miles South from Elgin)

- Pronunciation: Craig-al-a-kee
- Name Origin: Gaelic - "Rock of the stony place."
- Established: 1891.
- Location: Hill Street, Craigellachie, Aberlour.
- Region: Speyside.
- Visitor Center/Tours: Go to website for information.
- Website:www.craigellachie.com

Macallan Distillery (14 miles South from Elgin)

- Pronunciation: Mac-Allan.
- Name Origin: Gaelic - "Son of Allan."
- Established: 1824.
- Location: Easter Elchies, Aberlour.
- Region: Speyside.
- Visitor Center/Tours: Go to website for information.
- Website:www.themacallan.com

Aberlour Village (Pop. 1,000)
(15 miles South of Elgin)

Famous for its produce, Aberlour single malt whisky and Walker's Shortbread.

- Hotels, B&Bs, Food, Drink, Buses, Taxis, Shops, ATMs/Banks, Museums, Hospital, **Gas (petrol) & Charging Stations**.

Aberlour Highland Games

- Held in Early-August each year. Tossing the Caber, Highland dancing, Athletics, and Pipe bands.
  https://aberlourhighlandgames.co.uk
  Aberlour High School, Aberlour.

The Mash Tun Restaurant.

- Huge selection of whiskies included in this selection is the exclusive Glenfarclas Family Cask Collection. The Family Casks are a unique collection of 44 single cask whiskies, with one for each consecutive year from 1952 to 1995. The collection is unique as there is no other known collection of rare and old whiskies that covers 44 consecutive years from the same distillery.
  www.mashtun-aberlour.com
  8 Broomfield Square, Aberlour.

Aberlour Distillery (16 miles South from Elgin)

- Pronunciation: Abur-Lauer.
- Name Origin: Named after the town of Aberlour (Gaelic - Obar Lobhair).
- Established: 1826.
- Location: In the town of Aberlour.
- Region: Speyside.
- Visitor Center/Tours: Go to website for information.
- Website:www.aberlour.com

Balvenie Distillery(17 miles South from Elgin)

- Pronunciation: Bal-ven-y.
- Name Origin: Balvenie castle, located less than a mile away.
- Established: 1892.
- Location: Dufftown.
- Region: Speyside.
- Visitor Center/Tours: Go to website for information.
- Website:www.thebalvenie.com

Dufftown Highland Games (17 miles South from Elgin)

- Held in Late-July each year. Tossing the Caber, Highland dancing, Athletics, and Pipe bands.
  www.dufftownhighlandgames.com
  Mortlach Community Field, Hill Street, Dufftown.

Balvenie Castle (18 miles South from Elgin)

- Imposing 13th-century castle ruin with curtain wall and 16th century lodging. www.historicenvironment.scot *Castle Road, Dufftown.*

GlenAllachie Distillery(17 miles South from Elgin)

- Pronunciation: Glen-al-a-kee
- Name Origin: Gaelic - "The glen of the rocky place."
- Established: 1967.
- Location: Aberlour, Banffshire.
- Region: Speyside.
- Visitor Center/Tours: Go to website for information.
- Website: https

Dailuaine Distillery(18 miles South from Elgin)

- Pronunciation: Dal - Yewan.
- Name Origin: Gaelic - "The Green Meadow."
- Established: 1852.
- Location: Daugh of Kinermony, Aberlour.
- Region: Speyside.
- Visitor Center/Tours: Go to website for information.
- Website:www.malts.com/en-row/our-whisky-collection/dailuaine

Glenfiddich Distillery (18 miles South from Elgin)

- Pronunciation: Glen-Fidd-ik.
- Name Origin: Gaelic - "Valley of the deer."
- Established: 1886.
- Location: Dufftown, Keith.
- Region: Speyside.
- Visitor Center/Tours: Go to website for information.
- Website:www.glenfiddich.com

Benrinnes Distillery (19 miles South from Elgin)

- Pronunciation: Ben-rin-ness.
- Name Origin: Gaelic - "Promontory Hill."
- Established: 1835.
- Location: Aberlour.
- Region: Speyside.
- Visitor Center/Tours: Go to website for information.
- Website: No website at this time.

Dalmunach Distillery(19 miles South from Elgin)

- Pronunciation: Dal-mun-ak
- Name Origin: Named for the nearby pool in the River Spey.
- Established: Originally the Imperial distillery built in 1897 and demolished in 2013 and a new distillery built on the same site in 2014.
- Location: Carron, Moray.
- Region: Speyside.
- Visitor Center/Tours: Go to website for information.
- Website: No website.

Dufftown Distillery(19 miles South from Elgin)

- Pronunciation: Duff-tin
- Name Origin: Named for the town, which was named after its founder James Duff.
- Established: 1896.
- Location: Dufftown, Keith.
- Region: Speyside.
- Visitor Center/Tours: Go to website for information.
- Website:www.malts.com/en-us/our-whisky-collection/the-singleton-of-dufftown

Cardhu Distillery(20 miles South from Elgin)

- Pronunciation: Car-doo
- Name Origin: Gaelic - “Black Rock.”
- Established: 1811.
- Location: Knockando, Aberlour.
- Region: Speyside.
- Visitor Center/Tours: Go to website for information.
- Website:www.malts.com/en-gb/visit-our-distilleries/cardhu

Glenfarclas Distillery (20 miles South from Elgin)

- Pronunciation: Glen-Far-class
- Name Origin: Gaelic - "Valley of the green grass."
- Established: 1836.
- Location: Ballindalloch.
- Region: Speyside.
- Visitor Center/Tours: Go to website for information.
- Website: https

Tamdhu Distillery (21 miles South from Elgin)

- Pronunciation: Tam-doo.
- Name Origin: Gaelic - "Black hill."
- Established: 1896.
- Location: Knockando, Aberlour.
- Region: Speyside.
- Visitor Center/Tours: Go to website for information.
- Website:www.tamdhu.com

Ballindalloch Castle (23 miles South from Elgin)

- The Castle has been the home of the Macpherson-Grant family since it was finished in 1546.
  www.ballindallochcastle.co.uk
  Banffshire, Ballindalloch.

Cragganmore Distillery (25 miles South from Elgin)

- Pronunciation: Crag-an-more
- Name Origin: Gaelic - "The Big Rock."
- Established: 1870.
- Location: Cragganmore, Ballindalloch.
- Region: Speyside.
- Visitor Center/Tours: Go to website for information.
- Website:www.malts.com/en-us/visit-our-distilleries/cragganmore

Tormore Distillery (26 miles South from Elgin)

- Pronunciation: Tor-More
- Name Origin: Gaelic - "High hill."
- Established: 1958.
- Location: Richardson Road, Advie, Grantown-on-Spey.
- Region: Speyside.
- Visitor Center/Tours: Go to website for information.
- Website:www.tormoredistillery.com

Glenlivet Distillery(28 miles South from Elgin)

- Pronunciation: Glen-live-it.
- Name Origin: Gaelic - "Valley of the smooth place."
- Established: 1824.
- Location: Glenlivet, Ballindalloch.
- Region: Speyside.
- Visitor Center/Tours: Go to website for information.
- Website:www.theglenlivet.com

Tamnavulin Distillery (31 miles South from Elgin)

- Pronunciation: Tam-na-Voo-Lin
- Name Origin: Gaelic - "Mill on the hill."
- Established: 1966.
- Location: Tomnavoulin, Ballindalloch.
- Region: Speyside.
- Visitor Center/Tours: Go to website for information.
- Website:www.tamnavulinwhisky.com

Granton on Spey Highland Games (34 miles South from Elgin)

- Held in Late-August each year. Tossing the Caber, Highland dancing, Athletics, and Pipe bands.
  www.visitgrantown.co.uk
  Heithfield Park, Grantown on Spey.

Craggan Outdoors (36 miles South from Elgin)

- Archery, Clay Pidgeon Shooting, Climbing, Abseiling, Disc Golf, Fishing, Golf, Gorge Walking, Kayaking, Laser Tag, Mini Quads, Mountain Biking, Paintball, Pony Trekking, White Water Rafting, Ziplines.
  https://cragganoutdoors.co.uk
  Craggan Golf Course, Grantown-on-Spey.

Tomintoul Distillery(37 miles South from Elgin)

- Pronunciation: Tom-in-Towel.
- Name Origin: Gaelic - "Little hill of the barn."
- Established: 1964.
- Location: Tomintoul, Ballindalloch.
- Region: Speyside.
- Visitor Center/Tours: Go to website for information.
- Website:www.tomintoulwhisky.com

Tomintoul Highland Games (37 miles South from Elgin)

- Held in Late-July each year. Tossing the Caber, Highland dancing, Athletics, and Pipe bands.
  www.tomintoulhighlandgames.co.uk
  Tomintoul.

East from Elgin

Gordon Castle Highland Games (11 miles East from Elgin)

- Held Mid-May each year at the castle. Tossing the Caber, Highland dancing, Athletics, and Pipe bands.
  www.gordoncastle.co.uk/highland-games
  Gordon Castle Gordon Castle Estate, Fochabers.

Glen Keith Distillery (17 miles East from Elgin)

- Pronunciation: Glen-Keith.
- Name Origin: Gaelic - "Valley of the wood."
- Established: 1959.
- Location: Station road, Keith.
- Region: Speyside.
- Visitor Center/Tours: Go to website for information.
- Website:www.whisky.com/whisky-database/distilleries/details/glen-keith.html

Strathisla Distillery(17 miles East from Elgin) (3rd oldest distillery in Scotland.)

- Pronunciation: Strath-Eye-Lah.
- Name Origin: Gaelic - "Valley of the river Isla."
- Established: 1786.
- Location: Seafield Avenue, Keith.
- Region: Speyside.
- Visitor Center/Tours: Go to website for information.
- Website:www.maltwhiskydistilleries.com/strathisla

Strathmill Distillery (17 miles East from Elgin)

- Pronunciation: Strath-Mill
- Name Origin: Gaelic - "Valley of the mill."
- Established: 1891.
- Location: Keith.
- Region: Speyside.
- Visitor Center/Tours: Go to website for information.
- Website:www.malts.com/en-row/our-whisky-collection/strathmill

Glenglassaugh Distillery (25 miles East from Elgin)

- Pronunciation: Glen-Glass-au.
- Name Origin: Gaelic - "Valley of the Grey/green Place."
- Established: 1875.
- Location: Portsoy, Banff.
- Region: Speyside.
- Visitor Center/Tours: Go to website for information.
- Website:www.glenglassaugh.com

N

W E

S

West from Elgin

Miltonduff Distillery (3 miles West from Elgin)

- Pronunciation: Milton-Duff.
- Name Origin: Gaelic - "Duff's farm."
- Established: 1824.
- Location: Lochiepots Road, Elgin.
- Region: Speyside.
- Visitor Center/Tours: Go to website for information.
- Website: No website at this time.

Glenburgie Distillery (9 miles West from Elgin)

- Pronunciation: Glen-Bur-gy.
- Name Origin: Gaelic - "Glen of the fort."
- Established: 1810.
- Location: Alves, Moray
- Region: Speyside.
- Visitor Center/Tours: Go to website for information.
- Website: No website at this time.

Forres Highland Games (12 miles West from Elgin)

- Held in Early-July each year. Tossing the Caber, Highland dancing, Athletics, and Pipe bands.
  www.forreshighlandgames.com
  2002 Clovenside Road, Forres.

Benromach Distillery(13 miles West from Elgin)

- Pronunciation: Ben-rome-ak
- Name Origin: Gaelic - "Shaggy Mountain."
- Established: 1898.
- Location: Invererne Road, Forres, Moray.
- Region: Speyside.
- Visitor Center/Tours: Go to website for information.
- Website:www.benromach.com

Chapter 5

Kintyre and the West

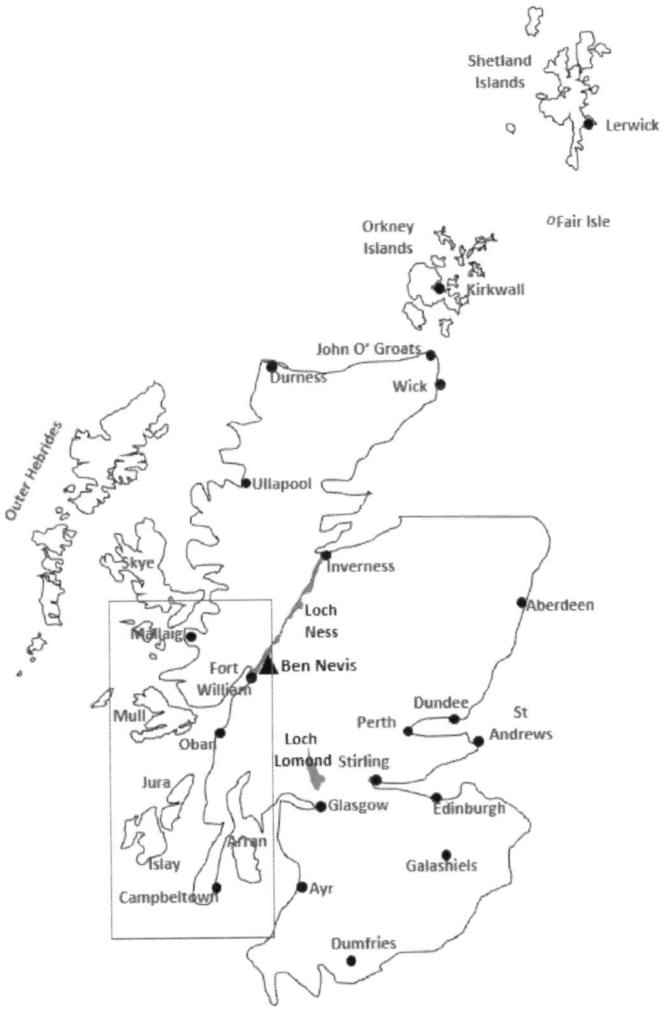

Arran,Campbeltown, Fort William, Islay, Oban & Mallaig.

The Isle of Arran(Pop. 5,000)

Often referred to as Scotland in miniature (20 miles north-south and 10 miles east-west), with mountains, glens, lochs, beaches and whisky. If you are bringing over a car, it's wise to fill your tank before you come. Gas (petrol) can be expensive on the isle and there are not that many Gas (petrol) stations. I am using Brodick as the start and finish point with distances from there, on a circular trip around the island (Counter-clockwise).

Getting there,by Ferry(the only option)

- From Ardrossan, Mainland to Brodick, Arran.
- From Campbeltown, Kintyre to Brodick, Arran.
- From Claonaig, Kintyre to Lochranza, Arran **Summer only.**
- From Tarbert, Kintyre to Lochranza, Arran **Winter only.** www.calmac.co.uk

Brodick(Pop. 600)

The main port and second biggest town.

- Hotels, B&Bs, Food, Drink, Car Hire, Buses, Taxis, Shops, ATMs/Banks, **Gas (petrol)& Charging Stations**.

Brodick Highland Games

- Held in Early-August each year. Tossing the Caber, Highland dancing, Athletics, and Pipe bands.
  www.facebook.com/BrodickHighlandGames
  Ormidale Park, Brodick.

Heritage Museum

- History, archaeology and geology of the isle.
  www.arranmuseum.co.uk
  Brodick.

Arran Brewery (2 miles from Brodick)

- Tours and tastings. See website for details.
  www.arranbrewery.co.uk

Brodick Castle (3 miles from Brodick)

- There has been a castle on this site for centuries, but the present building dates from 1844.

www.nts.org.uk/visit/places/brodick-castle-garden-country-park

Isle of Arran Distillery(14 miles from Brodick)

- Pronunciation: Ar-ran.
- Name Origin: Named for the island on which it is located.
- Established: 1995.
- Location: Lochranza, Isle of Arran.
- Region: Island.
- Visitor Center/Tours: Go to website for information.
- Website:www.arranwhisky.com

Lochranza Castle(14 miles from Brodick)

- Only a shell of the castle now remains, open to people and sheep.

The Sailor's Grave(15 miles from Brodick)

- In 1854 a sailor by the name of John McLean had died onboard ship and the crew wanted him buried in Lochranza, but the people were fearful that he may have had the plague, so refused.
  So, he was buried by the roadside outside of the village. It has become a custom to add a pebble to his grave if you stop there.

Auchagallon Stone Circle(9 miles from Brodick)

- A cross between a Cairn and a stone circle. This might be a good point to finish your day and head back to Brodick, if you are staying there, as you will have finished the top half of the island.

Kings Cave(11 miles from Brodick)

- Short walk from the parking area, sensible footwear recommended.
  https://forestryandland.gov.scot/visit/kings-cave

Machrie Moor Standing Stones(12 miles from Brodick)

- Can be a bit boggy under foot, so consider your footwear.

Blackwaterfoot(14 miles from Brodick)

- Hotels, B&Bs, Food, Drink, Buses, Taxis, Shops, ATM, **Gas (petrol)**.

Glenashdale Falls &Giants Graves(9 miles from Brodick)

- 3 miles circular walk to see the falls and the Giants graves (2 Neolithic chambered tombs).

Lamlash(Pop. 1,000)

The biggest town on the isle.

- Hotels, B&Bs, Food, Drink, Buses, Taxis, Shops, ATM, **Gas (petrol) & Charging Stations**.

Arran Coastal Way

A hiking circuit around the isle of Arran.
Distance: 66mi/109km
Duration: 10 days
Height Gain: 6863ft/2092m*
*This is dependent on whether you take in Goatfell mountain or any of the alternate routes or not.
www.coastalway.co.uk

Campbeltown (Pop. 4,800)

I am now using Campbeltown as the start point, with distances from there. We spent six days in Campbeltown while I was doing the Whisky School at the Springbank Distillery. As you head North, your options as to which direction to travel really open up; out to Islay, Jura, Mull and Iona or carry on up the West coast, turn off to the Cowal Peninsula or head into the mainland. From Campbeltown the route I have followed will take you to Oban, Fort William and finally Mallaig, with alternate routes shown, but always coming back to the North.

Getting there, Campbeltown Airport;

- From Glasgow
  www.hial.co.uk/campbeltown-airport

By Bus

- Citylink
  www.citylink.co.uk

By Ferry

- To/From Ardrossan.

- To/From Brodick, Arran.
  www.calmac.co.uk

Kintyre Express

- To/From Ballycastle Northern Ireland.
- To/From Port Ellen, Islay. https://kintyreexpress.com

Campbeltown

- Hotels, B&Bs, Food, Drink, shops, Buses, Taxis, Car Hire, ATMs/Banks, Hospital, Post Office, **Gas (petrol) & Charging Stations**. There a number of accommodations to be had in and around town, and out in the countryside. We stayed at the following hotel and would happily recommend it;

Ardshiel Hotel

- The food was superb, the whisky selection huge (over 700), and the staff very friendly. https://ardshiel.co.uk

Campbeltown Heritage Center

- Over 300 years of history from Campbeltown and the Kintyre Peninsula.

https://campbeltownheritagecentre.co.uk

Campbeltown Malts Festival

- Held annually every May. A 3-day celebration of Glengyle, Glen Scotia and Springbank. Campbeltown's 3 whisky distilleries. www.explorecampbeltown.com

Campbeltown Museum

- The story of Kintyre.

www.argyll-bute.gov.uk

Glen Gyle Distillery

- Pronunciation: Glen-Gile
- Name Origin: Gaelic - "Valley - Middle English *gyle*, from Middle Dutch *gijl*, to boil, ferment.
- Established: 2004.
- Location: Glengyle Road, Campbeltown.
- Region: Campbeltown.
- Visitor Center/Tours: Go to website for information.
- Website: https

Glen Scotia

- Pronunciation: Glen-Scosha.
- Name Origin: Gaelic - "Valley of the Scots."
- Established: 1832.
- Location: 12 High Street, Campbeltown.
- Region: Campbeltown.
- Visitor Center/Tours: Go to website for information.
- Website:www.glenscotia.com

Linda McCartney Memorial Garden

- Quiet garden in the center of town dedicated to Paul McCartney's late wife. www.lindasgarden.co.uk

Mull of Kintyre Music Festival

- Held annually every August in Campbeltown. www.explorecampbeltown.com

Mull of KintyreSea Tours

- Powerboat "Seafaris."

Springbank Distillery

- Pronunciation: Spring-Bank.
- Name Origin: Spring (water) from a bank.
- Established: 1828.
- Location: 9 Bolgam Street, Campbeltown.
- Region: Campbeltown.
- Visitor Center/Tours: Go to website for information.
- Website:http://springbank.scot

Springbank Whisky School

- Five-day school with hands on whisky making. http://springbank.scot/whisky-school

Davaar Island

- A tidal island reached by the *Dhorlin* shingle causeway at low tide. On the island is Stevenson lighthouse, and several caves with a painting of the crucifixion in one.

Heading North from Campbeltown

Sadell Abbey(10 miles from Campbeltown)

- Now aruin, thisCistercian monastery was in use between 1207-1507.

Beinn An Tuirc Distillery(13 miles from Campbeltown)

- Makers of Kintyre Gin.
  www.kintyregin.com
  Lephincorrach Farmhouse Torrisdale Castle Estate

Kennacraig Ferry Terminal(32 miles from Campbeltown)

- There's not much here, but there is a **Charging Station.**

- For ferries to Islay. www.calmac.co.uk

Side Trip East from Kennacraig

Skipness Castle(8 miles East from Kennacraig Ferry)

- 13th century castle and Chapel. www.historicenvironment.scot/visit-a-place/places/skipness-castle-and-chapel

We are about to take a detour to Islay from Kennacraig.

To continue on the route North, see page 306.

N

W E

S

Islay (Pop. 3,200)

(Pronounced Eye-la)

Across the sea to the West is "Isla, "known as the "Queen of the Hebrides," covering an area of 239 sq. miles, with nothing more than 18 miles from Bowmore, the capital. All distances will be shown from Bowmore. Islay is rightly famous for its whisky distilleries, details below. There is a wealth of accommodations to be had on Islay.

Getting there, Islay Airport;

- From, Edinburgh and Glasgow.
  www.hial.co.uk/islay-airport

- From Oban, mainland.
  www.hebrideanair.co.uk

By Ferry

- From Kennacraig, mainland to Port Ellen, Islay.

- From Kennacraig, mainland to Askaig, Islay.
  www.calmac.co.uk

Kintyre Express Ferry

- To/From Ballycastle, Northern Ireland (foot traffic only) to Port Ellen, Islay.

- To/From Campbeltown (foot traffic only) to Port Ellen, Islay.
  https://kintyreexpress.com

Cantilena Festival

- Chamber Music performed by Cantilena's professional musicians and students of the Royal Conservatoire of Scotland. Held annually in July at various venues on Islay.
  www.cantilenafestival.co.uk

Feis Ile

- Islay Festival with; Ceilidhs, Gaelic lessons, Golf, Music, Poetry and Whisky. Held annually at various venues across the isle in late May. www.islayfestival.com

Islay Jazz Festival

- Held annually in September at various venues on Islay.
www.islayjazzfestival.co.uk

Bowmore(Pop. 1000)

Famous for its whisky distillery (the 2nd oldest in Scotland). Next to the distillery is the MacTaggart Leisure Center whose swimming pool is warmed by Bowmore Distillery's surplus heat.

- Hotels, B&Bs, Food, Drink, Shops, Buses, ATMs/Banks, Post Office, **Gas (petrol) Station &Charging points.**

BowmoreDistillery(2nd oldest in Scotland)

- Pronunciation: Bo-more.
- Name Origin: Gaelic - Big Hut."
- Established: 1779.
- Location: School street, Bowmore.
- Region: Islay.
- Visitor Center/Tours: Go to website for information.
- Website:www.bowmore.com

Islay Whisky Academy

- Tours & Education. www.islaywhiskyacademy.scot

Kilarrow Church

- Known as the "Round Church" and built in 1769. www.undiscoveredscotland.co.uk/islay/roundchurch/index.html

Nerabus Gin Distillery (3 miles from Bowmore)

- Makers of Nerabus Islay dry gin. www.islayginltd.com

Bruichladdich Distillery(9 miles from Bowmore)

- Pronunciation: Brook-laddy.
- Name Origin: Gaelic - "The Bank of the Shore."
- Established: 1881.
- Location: Bruichladdich distillery, Islay.
- Region: Islay.
- Visitor Center/Tours: Go to website for information.
- Website:www.bruichladdich.com

*Bruichladdich and Kilchoman distilleries are close to each other.

Finlaggan(10 miles from Bowmore)

- The ruin of the home of the "Lords of the Isles" and looked upon as the "Cradle of Clan Donald."
  www.finlaggan.org

Museum of Island Life (10 miles from Bowmore)

- With items from the Mesolithic period (10,000 years ago) to 1950. www.islaymuseum.org

Port Ellen Village(10 miles from Bowmore)

- Hotels, B&Bs, Food, Drink, Shops, Bicycle& Electric Bicycle hire, buses, ATMs/Banks, Post Office, **Gas (petrol) Station &Charging points.**

Caol Ila (11 miles from Bowmore)

- Pronunciation: Cool-Eye-Lah.
- Name Origin: Gaelic - "Sound of Islay."
- Established: 1846.
- Location: Port Askaig, Islay.
- Region: Islay.
- Visitor Center/Tours: Go to website for information.
- Website:www.malts.com/en-gb/visit-our-distilleries/caol-ila

*Caol Ila, Ardnahoe and Bunnahabhain Distilleries are close to each other.

Islay Boat Trips (Port Askaig,11 miles from Bowmore)

- A variety of tours available, with the trip to the whirlpool of Corryvreckan, the 3rd largest in the world a highlight. When the tide is right, its roar can be heard ten miles away. www.islayinfo.com/islay-boat-trips.html

Ardnahoe Distillery(12 miles from Bowmore)

- Pronunciation: Ard-na-ho.
- Name Origin: "Height of the Hollow."
- Established: 2018.
- Location: Near Port Askaig, Islay.
- Region: Islay.
- Visitor Center/Tours: Go to website for information.
- Website: https://ardnahoedistillery.com

Kilchoman Distillery(12 miles from Bowmore)

- Pronunciation: Kil-Ho-Man
- Name Origin: Gaelic - "St Comman's church."
- Established: 2005.
- Location: Rockside Farm, Bruichladdich.
- Region: Islay.
- Visitor Center/Tours: Go to website for information.
- Website:https://kilchomandistillery.com

Laphroaig(12 miles from Bowmore)

- Pronunciation: La-Froy-g.
- Name Origin: Gaelic - "Hollow by the big bay."
- Established: 1815.
- Location: Laphroaig, Islay.
- Region: Islay.
- Visitor Center/Tours: Go to website for information.
- Website:www.laphroaig.com

*Laphroaig, Lagavulin and Ardbeg are close to each other.

Bunnahabhain Distillery(13 miles from Bowmore)

- Pronunciation: Boo-na-Hav-ven.
- Name Origin: Gaelic - "Foot (bottom) of the River."
- Established: 1883.
- Location: Bunnahabhain, Islay.
- Region: Islay.
- Visitor Center/Tours: Go to website for information.
- Website:https://bunnahabhain.com

Lagavulin (13 miles from Bowmore)

- Pronunciation: Lag-a-Voo-Lin.
- Name Origin: *Gaelic* - "Hollow of the Mill."
- Established: 1816.
- Location: Lagavulin, Islay.
- Region: Islay.
- Visitor Center/Tours: Go to website for information.
- Website:www.malts.com/en-gb/visit-our-distilleries/lagavulin

Islay Sea Adventures (Lagavulin,13 miles from Bowmore)

- A variety of tours available, with the trip to the whirlpool of Corryvreckan, the 3rd largest in the world a highlight. When the tide is right, its roar can be heard ten miles away. www.islayinfo.com/islay-boat-trips.html

Ardbeg (14 miles from Bowmore)

- Pronunciation: Ard-beg.
- Name Origin: Gaelic - "An Àird Bheag," meaning "The Small Promontory."
- Established: 1815.
- Location: Port Ellen.
- Region: Islay.
- Visitor Center/Tours: Go to website for information.
- Website:www.ardbeg.com

American Monument (15 miles from Bowmore)

- The monument was erected at the Oa (a rocky headland) in 1920 by The American Red Cross to commemorate the loss (close by) of American Sailors and Soldiers from two shipwrecks. www.lovefromscotland.co.uk/isle-of-islay-scotland

Kildalton Cross(18 miles from Bowmore)

- The Kildalton Cross is still standing where it was first erected more than 1,200 years ago, making it one of very few early Christian Celtic crosses still in their original position. www.historicenvironment.scot/visit-a-place/places/kildalton-cross

Jura (Pop. 200)

Just North of "Islay" is the Isle of "Jura," 30 miles long by 7 miles wide, with few people and around 7,000 Red Deer. Most visitors come here as part of a trip to nearby Islay. There is a bus service on Jura's one and only road, otherwise bring your own car or bicycle. Craighouse is the main village and has the only shop, hotel and pub on the island, the only two places to eat. Accommodation on Jura is limited, so if you wish to stay here, book early, your other option is to stay on Islay and come over on the ferry for a day trip. I am using the port of Feolin as the start point, with distances from there.

- Hotel, B&Bs, Self-Catering, Food, Drink, Shop, **Gas (petrol) Station.**

By Ferry(the only option, no need to book, pay onboard)

- From Askaig, Islay to Feolin, Jura. www.calmac.co.uk

Jura Boat Tours

- A variety of tours available, with the trip to the whirlpool of Corryvreckan, the 3rd largest in the world a highlight. When the tide is right, its roar can be heard ten miles away. www.juraboattours.co.uk

Jura Distillery(8 miles from Feolin)

- Pronunciation: Ju-Rah
- Name Origin: Old Norse - “Doirad’s Island.”
- Established: 1963.
- Location: Craighouse, Isle of Jura.
- Region: Island.
- Visitor Center/Tours: Go to website for information.
- Website:https://jurawhisky.com

Lussa Distillery(25 miles from Feolin)

- Makers of Lussa Gin. www.lussagin.com

Kennacraig &and the route North

Tarbert (Pop. 1300)

(5 miles North from Kennacraig Ferry)

My enduring memory of Tarbert, is from back in the late 70s. I was in the area with the Navy and was sitting in the "Frigate Bar" having a beer after hours. I looked to my left and there was a Police Sergeant, I thought we were all in trouble, but he took his hat off and ordered a whisky, fortunately he was off duty.
I will now use Tarbert as the start point, with distances from there.

- Hotel, B&Bs, Self-Catering, Food, Drink, Shops, ATM/Bank, Buses, Medical Center, **Gas (petrol) & Charging Station.** www.tarbertlochfyne.com

Ferry Terminal(Tarbert)

- From/to Portavadie.
  www.calmac.co.uk

Tarbert Castle Heritage Park

- The ruined structure of a medieval castle offers stunning views over the surrounding area. The Castle Heritage Park provides an excellent family picnic spot close to the village.

Scottish Series Yacht Regatta

- The second biggest yachting event in Britain, with several hundred yachts participating. Held Annually in May.
  www.tarbertlochfyne.com

Tarbert Music Festival

- Featuring contemporary and traditional Scottish Music. Held Annually in mid-September.
  www.tarbertlochfyne.com

Tarbert Seafood Festival

- Held Annually in the first full weekend of July. www.tarbertlochfyne.com

Stonefield Castle Hotel(2 miles from Tarbert)

- Scottish baronial styled castle dating back to 1837. www.bespokehotels.com/stonefieldcastle *Stonefield, Tarbert.*

Ardrishaig Village

(11 Miles from Tarbert)

- Hotel, B&Bs, Food, Drink, Shops, Post Office, ATM, Buses& Taxis.

Kilberry Sculptured Stones (15 Miles West from Tarbert)

- A collection of ancient grave markers.

Lochgilphead

(14 Miles North from Tarbert)

I will now use Lochgilphead as the start point, with distances from there.

- Hotel, B&Bs, Food, Drink, Hospital& Medical Center, Shops, Post Office, ATMs/Banks, Buses & Taxis.

From Lochgilphead you can head North/West or North/East

For the route North and West to Oban, Fort William and Mallaig see page318.

First the alternate route from Lochgilphead heading North/East, then South to the Isle of Bute.

Crarae Garden (14 Miles North from Lochgilphead)

- Waterfalls and Britain's finest example of a Himalayan-style garden. Visitor center, shop and café.
  www.nts.org.uk/visit/places/crarae-garden

Auchindrain (19 Miles North from Lochgilphead)

- A 22-acre museum, representing an important part of Scotland's past, showing how most people lived in Scotland prior to the 1700s. Containing the houses and other buildings of a small farming community known as a "**township**."
  www.auchindrain.org.uk

Inveraray (Pop. 600)

(25 Miles North East from Lochgilphead)

I will now use the town of Inveraray as the start point, with distances from there.

- Hotels, B&Bs, Food, Drink, Shops, ATM/Bank, Buses, **Gas (petrol) & Charging Station.**

Inveraray Jail

- Tour an old prison built in 1820. www.inveraryjail.co.uk

Inveraray Bell Tower

- Built to commemorate the members of Clan Campbell who died in the First World War. You can climb to the top for great views. www.inveraraybelltower.co.uk

Inveraray Castle

- Iconic castle and ancestral home of the Duke of Argyll, Chief of the Clan Campbell. www.inveraray-castle.com

Inveraray Highland Games

- Held in Mid-July each year. Tossing the Caber, Highland dancing, Athletics, and Pipe bands.
  http://inveraray-games.co.uk
  Inveraray Castle.

Dun Na Cuaiche watchtower (1 mile walk from Inveraray castle)

- Or you can drive almost all the way up, either way it's worth the effort for the view.
  www.inveraray-castle.com/walking

We now head around the top of Loch Fyne and down south to Dunoon and the Isle of Bute.

Benmore Botanical gardens (32 miles from Inveraray)

- 120-acre mountainside garden. www.rbge.org.uk/visit/benmore-botanic-garden

Dunoon (Pop. 4500)
(39 miles from Inveraray)

The main town on the Cowal Peninsula. There is a wealth of accommodations to be had in and around town.

- Hotels, B&Bs, Food, Drink, Shops, Museum, ATMs/Banks, Post Office **Gas (petrol) Station &Charging points.**

Getting there by Ferry

- Passenger Ferry - To/From Gourock (28 miles from Glasgow)
  www.calmac.co.uk

- Car Ferry - To/From McInroy's Point Gourock (30 miles from Glasgow)
  www.western-ferries.co.uk

Dunoon Highland Games

- Held in Late-August each year, this is the largest Highland gathering in the world. Tossing the Caber, Highland dancing, Athletics, and Pipe bands.
  www.cowalgathering.com
  Argyll Road, Kirn, Dunoon.

Castle House Museum

- The history of the Cowal peninsula, from Neolithic times to wartime. Enjoy a picnic in the beautiful gardens with views over the Clyde. https://castlehousemuseum.org.uk

Isle of Bute

Rothesay(Pop.6,000)

(Pronounced Roth – Say)

Rothesay is the main town and Ferry Port on the Isle.

- Hotels, B&Bs, Food, Drink, Shops, Museum, ATMs/Banks, Post Office, buses & Taxis, **Gas (petrol) Station &Charging points.**

Getting there by Ferry (32 miles from Glasgow)

- Passenger Ferry - To/From Weymss Bay (28 miles from Glasgow)
  www.calmac.co.uk

- Car Ferry - To/From Rhubodach, Bute/Colintraive, Cowal.
  www.calmac.co.uk

Bute Highland Games

- Held in late-August each year. Tossing the Caber, Highland dancing, Athletics, and Pipe bands.
  www.butehighlandgames.org
  The Stadium, High Street, Rothesay.

Bute Museum

- The history of Bute from Mesolithic and Neolithic times through to the closing years of the 20th century.
  www.butemuseum.org.uk

Rothesay Castle

- With a long association with the Stewart kings of Scotland.
  www.historicenvironment.scot

Mount Stewart House (4 miles from Rothesay)

- Magnificent Victorian gothic mansion. Home to the Stuarts of Bute, descendants of the Royal House of Stuart.
  www.visitbute.com/mount-stuart-house

Back to the North and West

(From Lochgilphead To Oban, Fort William& Mallaig)

The Dalriada Heritage Trail (3 Miles West from Lochgilphead)

- Linking the Crinan Canal, through ancient Atlantic oak woodlands with Achnabreac cup and ring marked rocks, Dunadd Fort, and the Moine Mhor National Nature Reserve through Kilmartin Glen (with standing stones and cairns) to Carnasserie Castle.

Dunadd Fort (5 Miles North from Lochgilphead)

- Dating back 2,000 years, then latterly royal power center for Gaelic kings in the 500s to 800s AD.
www.historicenvironment.scot

Dunchraigaig Cairn (7 Miles North from Lochgilphead)

- 4,000-year-old Bronze age burial mound.
www.historicenvironment.scot

Nether Largie Standing Stones (7 Miles North from Lochgilphead)

- Dating back almost 5,000 years. Nearby are also “Temple Wood stone rings” and “Nether Largie South Cairn.” www.britainexpress.com

Kilmartin Village(8 Miles North from Lochgilphead)

- Here in Kilmartin Glen, there is one of the richest concentrations of prehistoric monuments and historical sites in Scotland. Containing over 800 monuments within a 6-mile radius.

Kilmartin Museum

- With over 6, 000 years of History on display. Museum shop and a café. www.kilmartin.org

KilmartinCastle Hotel

- This 500-year-old Castle is now a luxury bed and breakfast venue. www.kilmartincastle.com

Carnasserie Castle(9 Miles North from Lochgilphead)

- Ruined 15th century tower house located a mile north of Kilmartin. www.visitscotland.com

Ardfern village (16 Miles North from Lochgilphead)

- Hotel (Galley of Lorne,17th Century Inn), B&Bs, Food, Drink, Craft Center with a tea-room, Shops, Buses and Yacht Benderloch Craignish was used the James Bond movie "From Russia with Love" for the motor-boat chase.

Craignish Cruises(17 Miles North from Lochgilphead)

- A variety of tours available, with the trip to the whirlpool of Corryvreckan, the 3rd largest in the world a highlight. When the tide is right, its roar can be heard ten miles away. www.craignishcruises.co.uk

Craobh Haven village (17 Miles North from Lochgilphead)

- Lord of the Isles Pub and Restaurant (live music), Shop, Yacht Center, Boat and Yacht Charters.

Jenny Wren Boat Adventures(17 Miles North from Lochgilphead)

- A variety of tours available, with the trip to the whirlpool of Corryvreckan, the 3rd largest in the world a highlight. When the tide is right, its roar can be heard ten miles away. www.jennywrenboatcharter.com/boat-trips

Lunga House Hotel (1 mile from Craobh Haven)

- 16th Century Tower House. www.lungahouse.co.uk

Arduaine Garden(20 Miles South from Oban)

- Tranquil exotic garden on the coast. www.nts.org.uk/visit/places/arduaine-garden

Clachan Bridge (The bridge over the Atlantic)
(12 Miles South from Oban)

- Old arched bridge (1793) joins the island of Seil to the mainland, spanning the Clachan Sound, which flows out of both ends into the Atlantic, giving it the nickname "The bridge over the Atlantic." As you cross the bridge, almost immediately on the right is an Inn called "Tigh an Truish" (Gaelic for The House of the Trousers). For a number of years after the 1745 Jacobite rebellion the British Government had banned the wearing of the kilt (the Act of Proscription).
  So, any islanders going over to work on the mainland would change out of their kilts here and into trousers, then change back on their return back to the island.
  www.atlasobscura.com/places/clachan-bridge-bridge-over-atlantic

The Scottish Slate Islands Heritage Trust(17 Miles South from Oban, 4 miles South from the Clachan Bridge)

- An interesting collection of artefacts and records relating to the social and industrial life of the Slate Islands of Argyll.
  https://slateislands.org.uk

Easdale Island(17 Miles South from Oban, 4 miles South from the Clachan Bridge)

- The World Stone Skimming Championships, held in late-September annually, open to the public. The island is reached by means of a 5-minute ferry from Ellenabeich on the Isle of Seil.
  www.stoneskimming.com

Easdale Island Folk Museum

- Featuring local life and history, with genealogical information available.
  www.easdalemuseum.org

The Puffer Bar, Restaurant and Tea-Room

- Award winning Bar & Restaurant on the tiny, car free island.
  http://pufferbarandrestaurant.co.uk

Oban (Pop. 8,500)

For many people the town of Oban is a stopover on their way to somewhere else, like the Western Isles. And yes, it can be, but it is also somewhere that deserves a few days to enjoy the town and its surrounding area. We stayed at the "Lodge House" Hotel, and can highly recommend it, with great food, great views and great staff. Oban is known as the seafood capital of Scotland.

- Hotels, B&Bs, Food, Drink, Shops, Museum, ATMs/Banks, Post Office, Buses & Taxis, **Gas (petrol) Station &Charging points.**

Getting there

- You can approach Oban by road from the South, East or North or you can get there by rail or bus.

Ferries to/from Oban

- To/From – Castlebay (Barra), Coll, Colonsay, Craignure (Mull), Kennacraig, Lismore, Lochboisedale (South Uist), Mallaig, Port Askaig (Islay), Tiree. Kerrera (from Gallanach, a jetty 3 miles south of Oban, a five-minute trip).
  www.calmac.co.uk

Oban Airport

- Flights to/from the islands of Coll, Colonsay, Islay and Tiree.
  www.hebrideanair.co.uk

Argyllshire Highland Games

- Held in Late-August each year. Tossing the Caber, Highland dancing, Athletics, and Pipe bands.
  www.obangames.com
  Mossfield Park, Oban.

Calmac Adventures

- Boat trip; From Oban, take the ferry to Mull, and then onwards to the tiny island of Ulva, lying just off Mull's west coast. From there, you'll continue on to Staffa.
  www.calmac.co.uk

Lorne Highland Games

- Held in Late-June each year. Tossing the Caber, Highland dancing, Athletics, and Pipe bands.
  http://lorne-highland-games.org.uk
  Oban.

McCaig's Tower

- Looking like a Scottish version of the Roman Colosseum, sitting atop Battery hill is McCaig's Tower. With gardens inside and views all around, well worth the steps to the top.

Oban Distillery(5th oldest distillery in Scotland).

- Pronunciation: Oh-bin.
- Name Origin: Gaelic - "Little bay."
- Established: 1794.
- Location: Stafford Street, Oban.
- Region: Highland.
- Visitor Center/Tours: Go to website for information.
- Website:www.malts.com/en-gb/visit-our-distilleries/oban

Oban Games &Argyllshire Gathering

- Highland games. Held annually on the fourth Thursday in August. https://obanlive.com

Oban Live

- Live music concert hosting the best of Scottish and international bands. Held annually in early June.
  https://obanlive.com

Oban War & Peace Museum

- Museum focusing on local life during peace and war.
  www.obanmuseum.org.uk

East from Oban

St Conan's Kirk (21 miles East of Oban)

- A beautiful church in a beautiful setting. The Kirk was consecrated in 1930 but has incorporated many pieces from older churches. The window in the Bruce chapel comes from a church in Lieth which was built in 1483, the ossuary contains a bone of King Robert the Bruce, beams in the cloister come from two wrecked Battleships HMS Caledonia and HMS Duke of Wellington and there are pieces of Iona Abbey built into the walls.
  www.stconanskirk.org.uk
  Lochawe, Dalmally.

Kilchurn Castle (23 miles East of Oban)

- One of the most photographed castles in Scotland. Built in the mid-1400s at the head of Loch Awe by Sir Colin Campbell, 1st Lord of Glenorchy.
  www.historicenvironment.scot
  Lochawe, Dalmally.

We are about to take a detour to the Isles of Mull and Iona.

To continue onthe route North for Fort William and Mallaig see page 336.

Isle of Mull (Pop. 3,000)

With 300 miles of coastline and hilly interior, Mull is both wild and beautiful. You will probably recognize the main town of Tobermory, from the harbor's brightly painted houses, a favorite on social media. You should probably fill your car in Oban before you head over to Mull as Gas/Petrol can be expensive on the isle. You have to travel through Mull to reach the nearby islands of Iona, Staffa (Fingal's Cave), and Ulva.

Ferries

- To/From –Oban to Craignure (Mull). Vehicle reservations are recommended. www.calmac.co.uk
- Iona to/from Fionnphort, Mull. On demand in the summer.

- Kilchoan, Ardnamurchan Peninsula to/from Tobermory, Mull. www.calmac.co.uk

- Lochaline, Morvern Peninsula to/from Fishnish, Mull. www.calmac.co.uk

- Ulva to/from Oskamull, Mull. The ferry runs on demand. www.calmac.co.uk

Tobermory(Pop. 1000)

If you have seen pictures of Scotland then you will probably recognize Tobermory's picture-perfect seafront, with the buildings painted in many bright colors.

- Hotels, B&Bs, Food, Drink, Shops, Aquarium, Museum, ATMs/Banks, Post Office, Buses & Taxis, **Gas (petrol) Station &Charging points.**

Mull Aquarium

- Europe's first catch and release aquarium. All creatures spend a maximum of 4 weeks in the aquarium before being returned to the sea. This means the exhibits are constantly changed.
  www.mullaquarium.co.uk

Mull Highland Games

- Held in Mid-July each year. Tossing the Caber, Highland dancing, Athletics, and Pipe bands.
  https://mullhighlandgames.weebly.com
  Erray Park, Tobermory.

Mull Museum

- The history of the Isle of Mull.
  www.mullmuseum.org.uk

Tobermory Distillery

- Pronunciation: Toe-Ber-More-ay.
- Name Origin: Gaelic - "Mary's well."
- Established: 1798.
- Location: Tobermory, Isle of Mull.
- Region: Island.
- Visitor Center/Tours: Go to website for information.
- Website: https

Staffa Tours

- Boat trips leaving from Tobermory (Mull), Fionnphort (Mull) and Iona to the isle of Staffa and Fingal's Cave.
  www.staffatours.com

Staffa Trips

- Boat trips leaving from Fionnphort (Mull) and Iona to the isle of Staffa and Fingal's Cave.
  www.staffatrips.co.uk

Glengorm Castle Hotel(5 miles from Tobermory)

- Dating from 1860, in the Scottish Baronial style.
  www.glengormcastle.co.uk
  Glengorm Castle, Tobermory.

Craignure(21 miles from Tobermory)

- Village and main ferry terminal. Hotel, B&Bs, Food, Drink, Shop, Car Hire, Post Office, Buses, **Charging points.**

Duart Castle(24 miles from Tobermory, 2 miles from Craignure)

- The seat of the Maclean family for the last 700 years.
  https://duartcastle.com

Iona(Pop. Less than 200)

The island is only 3.5 miles long by 1.5 miles wide, with the main settlement of “Baile Mor” (meaning "big town") consisting of a few cottages. The main reason tourist come to Iona is to see the Abbey founded by St Columba and built in 563.Cars are not allowed on Iona and the car park next to the ferry terminal in Fionnphort (Mull) is expensive. There is however a free car park at the back of Fionnphort village, but it's small and fills up quickly during the summer. Limited accommodation is available on Iona.

- B&Bs, Food, Drink, Shop, Museum, Post Office, Taxi (one).

Ferries

- Iona to/from Fionnphort, Mull. On demand in the summer.

Iona Abbey

- 6th century abbey founded by St Columba and where the famous book of Kells was written. The Abbey Museum houses Scotland's finest collection of early medieval carved stones and crosses.
  www.historicenvironment.scot

Iona Heritage Center

- Showcasing island life over the last few centuries; the fishing and crofting community, artists, churches, craftworkers, and memorable events. With a café and gift shop.
  www.ionaheritage.co.uk

Staffa Tours

- Boat trips leaving from Tobermory (Mull), Fionnphort (Mull) and Iona to the isle of Staffa and Fingal's Cave.
  www.staffatours.com

Staffa Trips

- Boat trips leaving from Fionnphort (Mull) and Iona to the isle of Staffa and Fingal's Cave.
  www.staffatrips.co.uk

We now rejoin the route North from Oban to Fort William.

Dunstaffnage Castle and Chapel(4 miles North from Oban)

- A MacDougal clan stronghold built around 1240 and taken by Robert the Bruce in 1308.Its most famous prisoner has to be Flora MacDonald held here in 1746 before being sent to the Tower of London for helping Bonnie Prince Charlie evade the Redcoats after Culloden.
  www.historicenvironment.scot

Castle Stalker(18 miles North from Oban)

- Iconic 15th century castle set in the middle of a Lochte castle is privately owned, but a limited number of tours are available by prior appointment. Go to website for details.
  www.castlestalker.com

Glencoe Village

(34 miles North from Oban, 17 miles from Fort William)

Named for the stunning Glen in which it sits and well known for the massacre of the Macdonalds in 13 Feb 1692 by government troops.

- Hotels, B&Bs, Food, Drink, Shop, Buses& Taxis, **Gas/Petrol &Charging points.**

Glencoe folk Museum (34 miles North from Oban, 17 miles from Fort William)

- Set within traditional 18th century heather-thatched cottages, Glencoe Folk Museum holds an eclectic array of objects celebrating local heritage and history. A 3-minute walk will get you to the Glencoe Memorial. www.glencoemuseum.com

Glencoe Memorial(34 miles North from Oban, 17 miles from Fort William)

- Memorial to remember the 38 Macdonald's massacred by British government soldiers on the13 Feb 1692.

Glencoe Outdoor Center

- Activities (depending on the season) include skiing, hill walking, climbing & abseiling, archery, orienteering, sailing, windsurfing, kayaking, and canoeing. www.glencoeoutdoorcentre.org.uk

Glencoe Visitor Center(35 miles North from Oban, 16 miles from Fort William)

- National Trust for Scotland visitor center, with information on the area. https://discoverglencoe.scot

Fort William(Pop. 10,500)

The town sits under the tallest mountain in the UK, Ben Nevis. Hiking to the top of Ben Nevis is a popular thing to do but be aware on a nice day it can take you 5 hours to get to the top. The path is rough (wear good shoes) and the weather can change, this is not to be taken lightly.
Fort William is known as the Outdoor capital of Scotland with lots of activities (depending on the season) that include skiing, hill walking, climbing (indoor and outdoor& abseiling, orienteering, archery, wind surfing, paddle boarding, biking, sailing, kayaking, and canoeing. Fort William is the start/Finish of the West Highland Way (97-mile hike from Milngavie, Glasgow) long distance walking route and also the start/Finish of the Great Glen Way (84-mile hike to Inverness) long distance walking route, I have hiked both routes (the WHW 7 times) and have written a guide to both.

- Hotels, B&Bs, Food, Drink, Shops, Museum, ATMs/Banks, Car Hire, Buses, Taxis, Post Office **Gas/petrol Station &Charging points.**

Getting there

- You can approach Fort William by road from the South, East or North or you can get there by rail or bus.

There is a wealth of accommodations to be had in and around town, and out in the countryside (all fall within the area marked on the map).
We have stayed at the following hotels and would happily recommend all of them;

Distillery Guest house

- Three former distillery workers cottages converted into a hotel. When we arrived, they gave us a glass of Whisky.
www.distilleryguesthouse.com

Lime Tree an Ealdhain

- Historic 1850 former Church Manse building overlooking the Loch in the center of Fort William
www.limetreefortwilliam.co.uk

Nevis Bank Inn

- Modern **hotel** situated 10 minutes' walk from the high street and the train station.
www.nevisbankinn.co.uk

Factor's Inn & Cottage(3 miles from Fort William)

- On Inverlochy Estate, staying here gives you access to Castle Hotel (Restaurant, high Tea etc.) at about a fifth of the price of staying at the castle. https://factorsinn.com

The Moorings, Banavie(3 miles from Fort William)

- Situated on the banks of the Caledonian Canal at the famous Neptune's staircase locks. Just five minutes' drive from Fort William town center but a million miles away from every-day hustle and bustle. https://moorings-fortwilliam.co.uk

While Hiking the Great Glen Way from Fort William to Inverness.

Aoanach Mor Hotel, Spean Bridge(9 miles from Fort William)

- Situated in the village of Spean Bridge, this is a delightful family-run hotel. www.aonachmorhotel.co.uk

Glengarry Castle Hotel(24 miles from Fort William)

- This 19th century country house sits in 60 acres on Loch Oich. www.glengarry.net

The Inch Hotel, Fort Augustus(24 miles from Fort William)

- The Inchnacardoch House was built by Lord Lovat as a hunting lodge over 150-years-ago. https://inchhotel.com

Glenmoriston Arms Hotel(38 miles from Fort William)

- A stone's throw from Loch Ness in the picturesque Highland village of Invermoriston. http://glenmoristonarms.co.uk

Urquhart Castle (48 miles East from Fort William)

- Dating way back to its start as a Pictish fort, this huge castle sits on a promontory dominating Loch Ness. www.historicenvironment.scot *Drumnadrochit, Inverness.*

Loch Ness Lodge(51 miles East from Fort William)

- This hotel (built in 1740) is located in the village of Drumnadrochit close to Loch Ness. We stayed here while hiking the Great Glen Way and can recommend it. www.lochnesslodgehotels.co.uk *Drumnadrochit.*

While Hiking the West Highland Way from Milngavie (Glasgow) to Fort William.

Clachaig Inn, Ballachuilish(20 miles from Fort William)

- Very popular with hikers and climbers. Dating back at least to 1864, this inn has a huge range of **Scottish craft ales**, lagers, stouts and ciders, a collection of over **400 malt whiskies,** over **130 Scottish distilled gins** amongst and ever-growing list of **Scottish rums, vodkas and other spirits.** https://clachaig.com

Bridge of Orchy Hotel(40 miles from Fort William)

- The Hotel has 32 rooms decorated in a traditional style and overlook the surrounding countryside. www.bridgeoforchy.co.uk

The Drovers Inn(57 miles from Fort William)

- The inn is over 300 years old and very likely had the famous Scottish outlaw Rob Roy as a patron, as this was the area from which he came.
  www.droversinn.co.uk

Crannog Cruises

- Leisurely cruises on Loch Linne.
  https://fortwilliamseatours.co.uk

Fort William Sea Tours

- Powerboat “Seafaris” on Loch Linne.
  https://fortwilliamseatours.co.uk

Jacobite Steam Train

- One of the most iconic train journeys in the world and of course made famous as the “Hogwarts Express” in the Harry Potter Movies.
  https://westcoastrailways.co.uk/jacobite/steam-train-trip

West Highland Museum

- Telling the story of the region and its history. With a collection relating to Bonnie Prince Charlie and the Jacobite cause. www.westhighlandmuseum.org.uk

Ben Nevis Distillery(2 miles North from Fort William)

- Pronunciation: Ben - Nevis.
- Name Origin: The highest mountain (Ben Nevis) in Scotland is next to the distillery.
- Established: 1825.
- Location: Lochy Bridge, Fort William.
- Region: Highland.
- Visitor Center/Tours: Go to website for information.
- Website:www.bennevisdistillery.com

Inverlochy CastleHotel(3 miles North from Fort William)

- This 19th century castle sits amongst the foothills of Scotland's highest mountain - the mighty Ben Nevis.
  https://inverlochycastlehotel.com
  Torlundy, Fort William.

Active Highs (22 miles North from Fort William)

- Outdoor Center with; Canyoning, Gorge Walking, Kayak Trips, Climbing & Abseiling, and White-Water Rafting.
  www.activehighs.co.uk
  The Great Glen Hostel, South Laggan, Spean Bridge.

East from Fort William

Glengarry Highland Games (16 miles East from Fort William)

- Held in Late-July each year. Tossing the Caber, Highland dancing, Athletics, and Pipe bands.
  https://glengarryhighlandgames.com
  A87, Invergarry.

Glenurquhart Highland Games (51 miles East from Fort William)

- Held in Late-August each year. Tossing the Caber, Highland dancing, Athletics, and Pipe bands.
  www.glenurquhart-highland-games.co.uk
  Drumnadrochit, Inverness.

West from Fort William

Neptune's Staircase (3 miles West from Fort William)

- Flight of 8 Locks on the Caledonian Canal at Banavie. www.scottishcanals.co.uk/locations/neptunes-staircase

Treasures of the Earth(4 miles West from Fort William)

- Museum with a unique collection of crystals and gems. https://treasuresoftheearth.co.uk

Glenfinnan Monument (17 miles West from Fort William)

- Monument to those that fell during the Jacobite rising of 1545/6. Glenfinnan is where Bonnie Prince Charlie raised his standard to start the rebellion. Standing at the head of Loch Shiel and set in stunning highland scenery, this is well worth your time. Also, just opposite is the famous Glenfinnan Viaduct, made famous in the Harry Potter films.
  www.nts.org.uk/visit/places/glenfinnan-monument
  Glenfinnan.

Glenfinnan Highland Games(17 miles West from Fort William)

- Held in Late-August each year. Tossing the Caber, Highland dancing, Athletics, and Pipe bands.
  www.glenfinnan.org.uk/gathering.asp
  Games Field, Glenfinnan.

Glenfinnan Station Museum (17 miles West from Fort William)

- Telling the story/history of the West Highland railway.
  https://glenfinnanstationmuseum.co.uk
  Glenfinnan.

Glenfinnan Viaduct (17 miles West from Fort William)

- Made famous in the Harry Potter films. *Glenfinnan.*

Arisaig Sea Kayak Center(36 miles North/West from Fort William)

- As the name suggests, offering Sea kayak adventures. https://arisaigseakayakcentre.co.uk *Arisaig.*

Arisaig Highland Games &Clan Donald Gathering (36 miles North/West from Fort William)

- Held in Late-July each year. Tossing the Caber, Highland dancing, Athletics, and Pipe bands. www.arisaighighlandgames.co.uk *Arisaig.*

Mallaig& Morar Highland Games (40 miles North/West from Fort William)

- Held in Early-August each year. Tossing the Caber, Highland dancing, Athletics, and Pipe bands.
  www.facebook.com/MallaigAndMorarHighlandGames
  Lovat Field, Morar.

Mallaig (Pop. 800)

(43 miles North/West from Fort William)

Mallaig is the main fishing port, a major ferry hub and the Rail terminus on the West coast of Scotland.

- Hotels, B&Bs, Food, Drink, Shops, Medical Center, Museum, ATM/Bank, e-bike hire, Buses, Post Office **Gas/petrol Station &Charging points.**

Getting there

- You can only approach Mallaig by road from the South/East or you can get there by rail or ferry. Scotrail provides a good service between Glasgow Queen Street to Fort William and Mallaig.

Ferries

- To/From Armadale, Isle of Skye.
  www.calmac.co.uk
- To/From Inverie, Knoydart Peninsula.
  www.calmac.co.uk
- To/From Inverie, Knoydart Peninsula.
  https://westernislescruises.co.uk
- To/From Lochboisdale, South Uist.
  www.calmac.co.uk
- To/From Oban.
  www.calmac.co.uk
- To/From the Isle of Eigg.
  www.calmac.co.uk
- To/From the Isle of Canna.
  www.calmac.co.uk
- To/From the Isle of Muck.
  www.calmac.co.uk
- To/From the Isle of Rum.
  www.calmac.co.uk
- To/From Tarbet.
  https://westernislescruises.co.uk

Mallaig Heritage Center

- Telling the story of West Lochaber, its people and landscape. Think Picts, Vikings and Scots. www.mallaigheritage.org.uk

Minch Adventures

- Opportunities to see whales, dolphins, seal colonies & sea eagles. www.minchadventures.co.uk

Chapter 6

The Western Isles

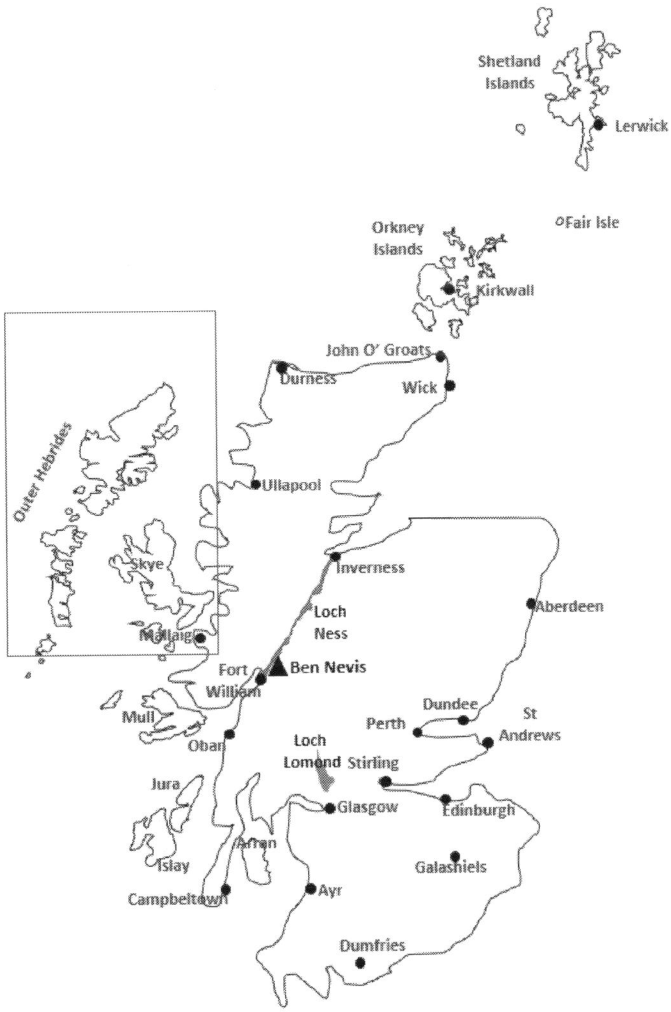

Hebridean Whisky Trail Festival

- Held in Late-May each year. With 4 distilleries situated on different Hebridean islands. https://hebrideanwhisky.com

HebCelt Festival

- Four-day Traditional Celtic Music Festival usually held in July at various venues on the Hebrides. www.hebceltfest.com

Isle of Skye(Pop. 10,000)

You can either cross over the Skye Bridge or get there by Ferry, I have done both. Arriving by ferry and leaving over the bridge.
The first night we stayed at the Rosedale hotel in Portree, which overlooks the harbor and was formerly three Fishermen's cottages. Our second night on Skye, we stayed at Kinloch Lodge, Sleat.
Skye is 639 sq. miles in area, but everything is less than 45 miles away from Portree.
Beautiful scenery, lots of wildlife and incredible seafood are all available here.

Getting there;

- Bridge from Kyle of Lochalsh – Kyleakin (Skye)
- Glenelg – Skye Ferry (Small with limited capacity. https://skyeferry.co.uk
- Mallaig – Armadale (Skye) www.calmac.co.uk/article/2982/Skye-Mallaig---Armadale

Things to do and see;

On our last trip, we caught the Ferry from Mallaig on the mainland to Armadale on Skye.
We did a circular tour around the island (by car), travelling counterclockwise.
The first night we stayed at the Rosedale hotel in Portree, which overlooks the harbor and was formerly three Fishermen's cottages.
Our second night on Skye, we stayed at Kinloch Lodge, Sleat. Leaving over the bridge to the mainland.

Armadale Castle, Gardens & Museum(42 miles from Portree)

- Unfortunately, the castle was ravaged by fire and only the shell remains, but the gardens make for a great walk and the museum is well worth a visit. www.armadalecastle.com

Torabhaig Distillery(38 miles from Portree)

- Pronunciation: To-ra-vaig.
- Name Origin: Named for the farm on which it was built.
- Established:2014.
- Location: Teangue, Isle of Skye.
- Region: Island.
- Visitor Center/Tours: Go to website for information.
- Website:www.torabhaig.com

Harapool & Broadford villages

(26 miles from Portree)

These two villages almost meld into one, they are so close together and they have;

- Hotels, B&Bs, Food, Drink, shops, ATMs/Banks, Post Office, Medical Center &**Gas (petrol) Station**.

Portree (Pop. 2,500)

The village of Portree (Port Ruighe in Gaelic) is the capital of Skye.

- Hotels, B&Bs, Food, Drink, shops, Car Hire, Bike Hire, ATMs/Banks, Post Office, **Gas (petrol)& Charging Stations**.

Isle of Skye Highland Games

- Held in Early-August each year. Tossing the Caber, Highland dancing, Athletics, and Pipe bands.
  www.skye-highland-games.co.uk
  Portree.

Isle of Skye Pipe band(Portree)

- Play every Tuesday evening in Somerled Square during the summer. www.spanglefish.com/isleofskyepipeband

The old Man of Storr(6 miles from Portree)

- The most famous (and busiest) walk on Skye, to one of the world's most photographed landscapes.

Kilt Rock & Mealt Falls(15 miles from Portree)

- Kilt Rock gets its name from the 90-meter-high Basalt rock cliff face that resemble the pleats in a kilt.

Quirang(19 miles from Portree)

- This can be hiked, but is quite difficult, with stunning scenery. In an area known as Trotternish.

You are about to turn around the top of the isle and the distances back to Portree will lessen.

The Skye Museum of Island life(22 miles from Portree)

- Giving an insight to island life 100-years-ago, well worth a visit.
  www.skyemuseum.co.uk

Flora McDonald's Grave

- Next to the Skye Museum of Island life.
  "Her name will be mentioned in history and if courage and fidelity be virtues, mentioned with honour."
  Alexander McQueen the famous fashion icon is also buried here.

Uig (16 miles from Portree)

- Village with; Food, drink, shop, Post Office &**Gas (petrol) Station.**

Fairy Glen(16 miles from Portree)

- Lovely landscape, which makes it easy to believe that Fairies inhabit the area.

Just after the village of Borve, take the A850 (Turn right) to carry-on around the isle.

Dunvegan Castle(22 miles from Portree)

- The Castle is the oldest continuously inhabited castle in Scotland and has been the ancestral home of the Chiefs of clan MacLeod for 800 years. www.dunvegancastle.com *MacLeod Estate, Dunvegan.*

Dunvegan

(20 miles from Portree)

- Village with shops &**Gas (petrol) Station.**

Possible Side Trip from Dunvegan

Three Chimneys Restaurant(5 miles from Dunvegan castle)

- Eating lunch here was our first experience of a Michelin starred restaurant and the price reflected it. But the food was stellar, as was the service. While we were waiting for our food, I looked out the window and saw Dolphins/Porpoises playing in Loch Dunvegan. www.threechimneys.co.uk

Neist Point Lighthouse(6 miles from The Three Chimney's)

- About a 45-minute-walk (round-trip) from the car park to one of Scotland's most famous and picturesque lighthouses.

Back to the route around Skye

Lonmore village(11 miles from Neist Point Lighthouse)

- At the village, turn right onto the A863 to carry-on around the isle.

Back to the route South

Talisker Distillery(19 miles from Lonmore)

- Pronunciation: Tal-isk-er
- Name Origin: Gaelic - "Sloping rock."
- Established: 1831.
- Location: Carbost, Isle of Skye.
- Region: Island.
- Visitor Center/Tours: Go to website for information.
- Website:www.malts.com/en-row/our-whisky-collection/talisker

Fairy Pools(20 miles from Portree)

- Beautiful pools that you can swim in (if you like really cold water) or you could just take some stunning photos.

Kinloch Lodge

- We finished our tour of Skye here, where we had dinner and stayed the night. The restaurant was also Michelin starred and again the food was superb and relatively inexpensive as it was rolled into the cost of the room. https://kinloch-lodge.co.uk

Outer Hebrides

(Western Isles)

All the major islands are connected to each other by Ferry. The Hebrides are famous for their white sandy beaches. If, you are travelling by car you must book your Ferry ticket in advance.
The remote locations, small populations and lack of light pollution on these islands make for great star gazing and viewing the northern lights (best in winter).
There is ample opportunity to walk/hike or bike and see the beautiful scenery, view the wildlife and work up an appetite for some incredible seafood.
I have laid out the Islands as you see them on a map, starting at the top with;

- Lewis
- Harris
- Berneray
- North Uist
- Benbecula
- South Uist
- Eriskay
- Barra

Isle of Lewis(Pop. 19,000)

The isles of Lewis (Northern) and Harris (Southern) are in fact one island, the largest in Scotland. Until the 20th century there were no roads between Lewis and Harris, because of the mountains on the island.
The only way to get from Lewis to Harris was by sea, hence them being classed as two separate islands. The isle of Lewis covers 683 sq. miles and for distances around the Isle, I am assuming a start point of Stornoway as it is the main town and ferry port of the isle.

Getting there, Stornoway Airport;

- From Benbecula, Edinburgh, Glasgow and Inverness (Logan Air) www.hial.co.uk/stornoway-airport

By Ferry

- From Ullapool to Stornoway.

- Oban to Lochboisdale, Isle of South Uist www.calmac.co.uk

Stornoway(Pop. 6,000)

The main town and port.

- Hotels, B&Bs, Food, Drink, Car Hire, Shops, ATMs/Banks, Post Office, **Gas (petrol)& Charging Stations**.

Bosta House

- Reconstruction of an Iron Age house found nearby. Guides are on hand to explain what it was like to live there.
  https://berneramuseum.wixsite.com

HebCelt Festival

- Four-day Traditional Celtic Music Festival usually held in July at various venues on the Hebrides.
  www.hebceltfest.com

Lewis Castle & Museum

- Built in 1847 and now home to the famous Lewis chessmen. Offering self-catering and hotel rooms.
  www.lews-castle.co.uk
  Stornoway.

The Blackhouse Arnol(15 miles from Stornoway)

- A "Blackhouse" was the standard type of house the islanders lived in around 100-years-ago. Close to Dun Carloway Broch, Callanish Standing Stones and Gearrannan Blackhouse Village and Shawbost Norse Mill and Kiln.

Callinish Standing Stones (17 miles from Stornoway)

- Impressive 5,000-year-old stone circle. Close to Dun Carloway Broch, Gearrannan Blackhouse Village and Shawbost Norse Mill and Kiln. www.historicenvironment.scot/visit-a-place/places/calanais-standing-stones

Dun Carloway Broch(18 miles from Stornoway)

- Stone tower built circa 200 BC. Close to Callanish Standing Stones, Gearrannan Blackhouse Village and Shawbost Norse Mill and Kiln. www.historicenvironment.scot/visit-a-place/places/dun-carloway

Gearrannan Blackhouse(18 miles from Stornoway)

- Village and living Museum with self-catering accommodation. Close to Callanish Standing Stones, Dun Carloway Broch, and Shawbost Norse Mill and Kiln.
  www.gearrannan.com

Shawbost Norse Mill and Kiln(19 miles from Stornoway)

- Close to Dun Carloway Broch, Callanish Standing Stones and Gearrannan Blackhouse Village.

Abhainn Dearg Distillery(36 miles from Stornoway)

- Pronunciation: Aveen Jarraek.
- Name Origin: Gaelic - "Red River."
- Established: 2008.
- Location: Carnish, Isle of Lewis.
- Region: Island.
- Visitor Center/Tours: Go to website for information.
- Website:www.abhainndearg.co.uk

Uig historical society Museum (33 miles from Stornoway)

- Local Historical Society Museum with several displays covering different aspects of local history. www.ceuig.co.uk

Isle of Harris(Pop. 21,000)

The isles of Lewis (Northern) and Harris (Southern) are in fact one island, the largest in Scotland. Until the 20th century there were no roads between Lewis and Harris, because of the mountains on the island. The only way to get from Lewis to Harris was by sea, hence them being classed as two separate islands. The isle of Harris covers 683 sq. miles and for distances around the Isle, I am assuming a start point of Tarbert as it is the main town and ferry port of the isle.

Getting there, Stornoway Airport;

- From Benbecula, Edinburgh, Glasgow and Inverness (Logan Air) www.hial.co.uk/stornoway-airport

By Ferry

- From Uig, Isle of Skye to Tarbert. www.calmac.co.uk

Tarbert (Pop. 500)

The main town and port.

- Hotels, B&Bs, Food, Drink, Car Hire, Shops, ATMs/Banks, Post Office, **Gas (petrol)& Charging Stations**.

Amhuinnsuidhe Castle Hotel(6 miles from Tarbert)

- Built in 1865 in the Scottish Baronial style. http://amhuinnsuidhe-com.stackstaging.com *Amhuinnsuidh.*

Bunavoneader Whaling Station (4 miles from Tarbert)

- No longer active, some remains can be seen like the Chimney and a few Whale bones. www.virtualheb.co.uk/whaling-station-isle-of-harris

Isle of Harris Distillery

- Pronunciation: Isle-of-Harris.
- Name Origin: Named for the Island where it is situated.
- Established:2015.
- Location: Tarbert, Isle of Harris.
- Region: Island.
- Visitor Center/Tours: Go to website for information.
- Website: https

Shawbost

- Harris Tweed Mill and shop. www.harristweedhebrides.com

St Clemens Church(6 miles from Tarbert)

- Built in the early 1500s, built as the burial place of the Clan MacLeod. www.historicenvironment.scot

Isle of Berneray(Pop. 137)

Covering an area of only around 6 sq. miles. There is a bus service from the isle of Berneray in the North, down through North Uist, Benbecula, and South Uist to the isle of Eriskay in the South, with causeways linking the islands.
The isle is probably best known for its beaches and coves, the West beach is 3 miles of un-spoilt sand.
If you wish to see the Northern lights, this is one of the best places to go, with no light pollution they can easily be seen (mainly in Winter).

Isle of North Uist(Pop. 1200)

The isle stretches 20 miles north-south, 25 miles east-west. For distances around the Isle, I am assuming a start point of Lochmaddy as it is the main village and ferry port of the isle. No car hire on the island, but you can book a car from Benbecula airport and have it dropped off, to meet you at the ferry. Taxis and minibuses are available, as well as the regular islands bus service.

Getting there, Benbecula Airport;

Benbecula is the small isle Lying between North and South Uist and linked to both by road causeways.

- From Glasgow, Inverness and Stornoway (Logan Air)
  www.hial.co.uk/benbecula-airport

By Ferry

- From Uig, Isle of Skye to Lochmaddy.
  www.calmac.co.uk

Lochmaddy

- The main town and port. Hotels, B&Bs, Food, Drink, Shops, ATMs, Post Office, **Gas (petrol)& Charging Stations**.

Camera Obscura(Hut of the Shadows)

- Go on a sunny day to see a projected view of Lochmaddy.

Taigh Chearsabhagh Museum & Arts Center

- Local art center, shop, Cafe and Post Office. www.taigh-chearsabhagh.org

Barpa Langass(6 miles from Lochmaddy)

- A 5000-year-old burial chamber. A short walk away is Pobull Fhinn.

Pobull Fhinn(6.5 miles from Lochmaddy)

- Stone circle from around 2,000BC. A short walk away is Barpa Langass.

The Hebridean Smokehouse (8 miles from Lochmaddy)

- With a long tradition of peat-smoking delicious seafood.
  www.hebrideansmokehouse.com
  Clachan.

Isle of Benbecula (Pop. 1300)

The small isle Lying between North and South Uist and linked to both by road causeways.
The isle stretches 7 miles north-south and 7 miles east-west. Car hire is available at the airport, best to pre-book.

Getting there, Benbecula Airport;

- From Glasgow, Inverness and Stornoway (Logan Air)
  www.hial.co.uk/benbecula-airport

Balivanich

The main village.

- Hotel, B&Bs, Self-Catering, Food, Drink, Shops, ATM/Bank, Post Office, **Gas (petrol)& Charging Stations**.

Isle of South Uist(Pop. 1800)

The isle stretches 25 miles north-south and 5 miles east-west. For distances around the Isle, I am assuming a start point of Lochboisedale as it is the main village and ferry port of the isle. South Uist is linked by a causeway to Eriskay in the South and to North Uist in the North.

Getting there, Benbecula Airport;

Benbecula is the small isle Lying between North and South Uist and linked to both by road causeways.

- From Glasgow, Inverness and Stornoway (Logan Air)
  www.hial.co.uk/benbecula-airport

By Ferry

- From Castlebay, Barra to Lochboisedale.
- From Mallaig to Lochboisedale.
- Oban to Lochboisdale.
  www.calmac.co.uk

Lochboisedale

The main Village and Port.

- Hotel, B&Bs, Self-Catering, Food, Drink, Shops, ATM/Bank.

South Uist Highland Gathering

- Held in Late-July each year. Tossing the Caber, Highland dancing, Athletics, and Pipe bands.
  www.shottshighlandgames.org.uk
  Askernish Machair, Nr Lochboisdale, South Uist, Outer Hebrides

Kildonan (7 miles Lochboisdale)

- Flora MacDonald's Birthplace.

- Museum with café and shop.
  https://kildonanmuseum.co.uk

Our Lady of the Isles (16 miles Lochboisdale)

- 30ft high statue in granite of the Madonna and Child.

Isle of Eriskay(Pop. 130)

The isle stretches 2.8 miles long north to south and 1.6 miles wide and is linked by a causeway to South Uist.
In 1941, the SS Politician ran aground in the waters between South Uist and Eriskay, with a cargo of whisky. This was the basis for the book and film Whisky Galore and the only pub on the island is called the "Politician" (food and drink). The island is also known for its native Eriskay Ponies.
There are several B&Bs on the island.

By Ferry

- From Barra to Lochboisedale. www.calmac.co.uk

Eriskay

The main Village.

- Hotel, B&Bs, Self-Catering, Food, Drink, Shops, Post Office.

Isle of Barra(Pop. 1100)

The isle is 11 miles long and 6 miles wide. For distances around the Isle, I am assuming a start point of Castlebay as it is the main village and main ferry port of the isle. Buses, Taxis, Car and Bike hire are available. Hotels and B&Bs are available throughout the isle.
The main road (A888) is circular and there are signs to monuments and villages.

Getting there, Barra Airport (9 miles from Castlebay)

- From Glasgow (Logan Air)
  Barra Airport is one of the last in the world that still uses a beach as its runway. A siren sounds when an aircraft is coming into land and you need to get clear of the beach.
  www.hial.co.uk/barra-airport

By Ferry

- From Oban to Castlebay, Isle of Barra.

- From Eriskay to Ardmhòr, Isle of Barra.
  www.calmac.co.uk

Castlebay Village

- Hotel, B&Bs, Food, Drink, Hospital, Bank/ ATM, Shops and **Gas (petrol)&Charging Stations.**

Dun Cuier(4.5 miles from Castlebay)&**Dun Bharpa**(4.2 miles from Castlebay)

- Old ruined hill forts (Brochs), of the two Dun Cuier is the better preserved. Access to both involves walking over rough ground and a bit of an ascent, with Dun Cuier the shorter walk.

Hebridean Toffee Company

- Gift shop and café with deck overlooking the bay.
  www.hebrideantoffeecompany.com
  Castlebay.

Isle of Barra Distillery

- Makers of "Atlantic Gin."
  www.isleofbarradistillers.com
  Castlebay.

Kisimul Castle (late 15th century)

- A 5-minute boat trip from Castlebay and open from April to September. The seat of the chief of Clan MacNeil.
Castlebay.

St Barr's Church(9.5 miles from Castlebay)

- Now a ruin, but in the north chapel is a full-size replica of an elaborate Norse rune stone which was found in the cemetery in 1865.
On one side the runic inscription reads "After Thorgerth, Steiner's daughter, this cross was raised," on the other side is an elaborate Celtic cross with plaited interlace.
There are also three 16th century grave-slabs in this chapel believed to have once covered the graves of the MacNeils.
www.visitouterhebrides.co.uk
1 Cille Bharra, Eoligarry.

Isle of Vatersay(Pop. 90)

The isle is only 3 miles from north to south, the northern section of the island is about 3 ½ miles from west to east and is linked by a causeway to Barra.
Accommodation; One self-catering cottage.

Dun a' Chaolais

- Remains of a Broch (fortified house/tower).

Chapter 7

The North and the North Coast 500

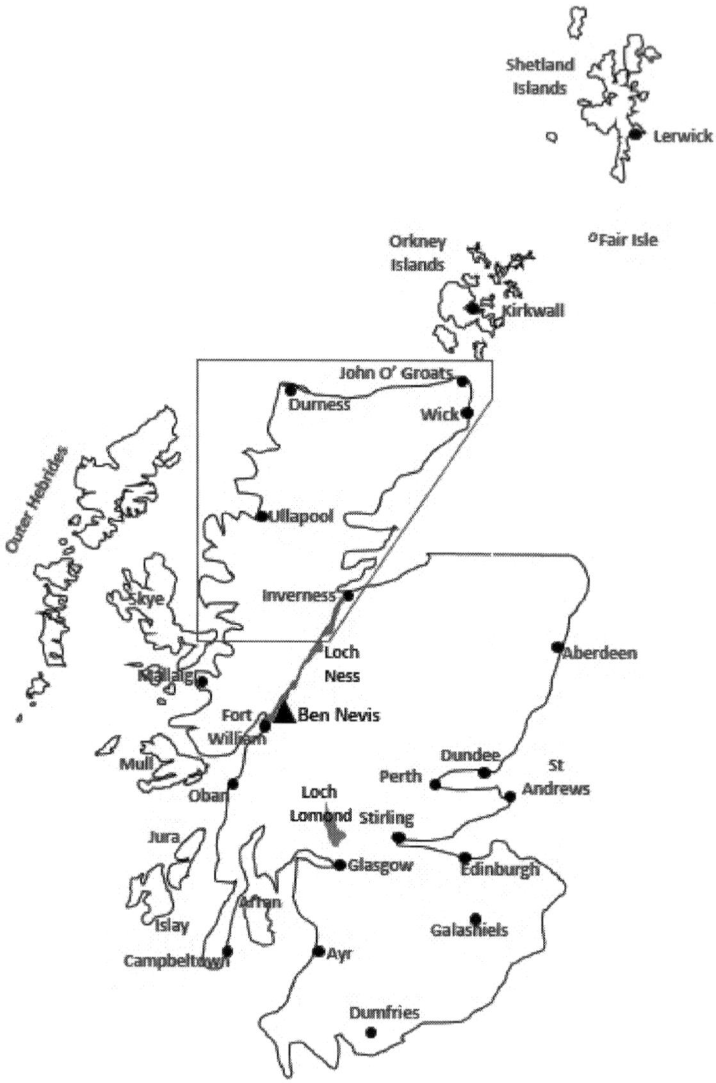

The Northern Highlands and the North Coast 500 are pretty much one and the same, with most of what you will want to see, along the coast. Yes, there are villages and Hamlets sprinkled through the center of the highlands and some great scenery. But there are no historic sites or specific things to do and see, as there are around the coast.
My recommendation is that you start and finish in Inverness, although it is a circular route, so it's up to you.
I suggest going clockwise around the North Coast 500 (NC500), as I believe the views are more spectacular if you go this way. The NC500 is basically a Coastal Route, so there are a lot of beautiful beaches. I'm not suggesting that you go swimming as it might be a little chilly, but I am suggesting that you bring shoes that you can walk over rough ground in, to get to the beaches.
There is a wealth of accommodations to be had in the Inverness, we stayed at the Palace Hotel (www.invernesspalacehotel.co.uk), which overlooks the river and has some nice restaurants within easy walking distance, or you could choose to eat in the hotel. The rest of the route does have accommodation, but nothing on the scale of Inverness. I therefore recommend that you book your accommodations early.

Highland Whisky Festival (NC500)

- Eight-day festival held in Mid-May each year. With 8 distilleries situated on the North Coast 500 each hosting a different day of the festival. www.highlandwhiskyfestival.co.uk

Inverness(Pop. 47,000)

Known as the capitol of the highlands, this Victorian town is a good base for you to travel the highlands.

- Hotels, B&Bs, Food, Drink, Shops, Museum, ATMs/Banks, Post Office **Gas (petrol) Station &Charging points.**

Around Inverness (Not on the NC500)

I recommend an extra day or two in Inverness, to visit Culloden Battlefield and to look around the town.

City of Inverness Highland Games

- Held in Late-July each year. Tossing the Caber, Highland dancing, Athletics, and Pipe bands.
  http://invernesshighlandgames.com
  Bught Park, Inverness.

Inverness Cathedral

- The cathedral was consecrated in 1874.
  https://moray.anglican.org/inverness-cathedral
  Ardross Street, Inverness.

Jacobite Cruises

- Your chance to spot the Loch Ness Monster.
  www.jacobite.co.uk
  Inverness.

Bunchrew House Hotel(4 miles to Inverness)

- Dating back to 1641 this Scottish mansion sits in beautiful gardens on the shores of the Beauly Firth.
  https://bunchrewhousehotel.com
  Bunchrew.

Strathconon Highland Games (32 miles from Inverness)

- Held in Late-July each year. Tossing the Caber, Highland dancing, Athletics, and Pipe bands.
  www.strathcononhall.co.uk
  Daybreak Games Field, Strathconon.

The NC500 route

Route of the North Coast 500 shown by the dotted line.

I have not suggested a fixed itinerary, as everyone is different in what they want to see and do. Instead I have broken the route up to show what is available to see and do in that section. Mileage is shown to the end, of each listed section.
I have also put things in the order you would come across them as you travel the North Coast 500. Each day would appear to be a short drive, but with so many hamlets, villages, towns, beaches, views, things to see/do and places to eat, that your day can quickly fill up.
I have outlined the highlights of the NC500 below, as I can't list everything, or this guide would need to be published in volumes.
I suggest that you book your accommodation well in advance, as this route is very popular and accommodation although not scarce, does fill up fast.
I have shown Gas (petrol) stations and charging stations on the route (in **Bold**).
I'm now going to state the obvious, if you are using a GPS, be aware that it will take you the most direct route. For instance; if you are starting the day in Ullapool and intend to finish the day at Wick, it will take you by the shortest route across country and you will miss about half of the NC500.
Look at the map and use your GPS for waypoints such as Durness, then John O' Groats etc.
Finally, it's your trip, take your time and be on the lookout for signs to things that interest you and drive safe, some of these country roads are narrow.

Highland Whisky Festival

- Eight-day festival held in Mid-May each year. With 8 distilleries situated on the North Coast 500 each hosting a different day of the festival. www.highlandwhiskyfestival.co.uk

Inverness to Applecross

(80 miles – 2 hrs.)

Glen Ord Distillery(66 miles to Applecross)

- Pronunciation: Glen-Ord.
- Name Origin: A plain called the Ord.
- Established: 1838.
- Location: The Black Isle near Inverness.
- Region: Highland.
- Visitor Center/Tours: Go to website for information.
- Website:www.malts.com/en-gb/visit-our-distilleries/glen-ord

Contin

(60 miles to Applecross)

- Village Store, B&B and **Gas (petrol) Station**.

Rogie Falls

(58 miles to Applecross)

- 3-minute walk, from the car park to the falls, trails are signposted.

Lochcarron

(17 miles to Applecross)

- Hotels, B&B, Shop, Food, Drink, Medical Center &**Gas (petrol) Stations**.

Lochcarron Highland Games

- Held in Late-July each year. Tossing the Caber, Highland dancing, Athletics, and Pipe bands.
  www.lochcarrongames.org.uk
  Attadale Estate, Lochcarron.

Bealach na Ba

(5 miles to Applecross)

- "Pass of the cattle" is an amazing road with great views across much of Wester Ross, the Isle of Skye, and the Islands of Rum and the Outer Hebrides. An unforgettable drive.

Applecross

- The name of the peninsula. The row of houses on "Shore Street" where the "Applecross Inn" is situated is often mistakenly called Applecross.

Applecross Inn

- With accommodation, food and drink. Around 60 whiskies and many Scottish Gins.
  Shore Street, Applecross.

Applecross to Ullapool

(112 miles – 3 hrs.)

Whether you travel back over the "Bealach na Ba" or go around the coast, both routes are 20 miles to Shieldaig.

Shieldaig

(92 miles to Ullapool)

- Hotel, B&Bs, Food, Drink.

The Torridon Hotel (87 miles to Ullapool)

- Scottish Hotel of the year 2011. With over 365 single malt whiskies on its shelves, the Whisky & Gin Bar also offers 120 Gins. **Charging points.**
  By Achnasheen.

Kinlochewe

(75 miles to Ullapool)

- Hotel, B&Bs, Food, Drink, Post Office &**Gas (petrol) Station**.

Gairloch Highland Gathering (23 miles West from Kinlochewe)

- Held in Late-June/early July each year. Tossing the Caber, Highland dancing, Athletics, and Pipe bands. www.shottshighlandgames.org.uk *Sands Caravan & Camping Gairloch, Wester Ross.*

Victoria Falls(64 miles to Ullapool)

- Named for Queen Victoria, who visited in 1877. A short walk from the car park.

Gairloch

(56 miles to Ullapool)

- Hotel, B&Bs, Food, Drink, ATM, **Gas (petrol) Station & Charging Points.**

Poolewe

(50 miles from Ullapool)

- Hotel, B&Bs, Food, Drink, &**Gas (petrol) Station**.

Inverewe Gardens(49 miles from Ullapool)

- Heritage garden, with plants from all over the world
  www.nts.org.uk/visit/places/inverewe
  Inverewe.

Aultbe

(44 miles from Ullapool)

- Hotel, B&Bs, Food, & Drink.

Loch Ewe Distillery (44 miles from Ullapool)

- With the smallest stills (2 x 120 litres each) of any legal distillery in Scotland. It was founded through a loophole in Scottish law, which was closed immediately after Loch Ewe was granted a license. Producing up to 600 litres of spirit per year, most of which is bottled after six weeks maturation as 'Spirit of Loch Ewe.'
  https://scotchwhisky.com
  Aultbe.

Suspension Bridge at the Corrieshalloch Gorge (12 miles from Ullapool)

- This Victorian, 82 feet long suspension bridge hangs over one of the most spectacular gorges in Britain

Ullapool

- Hotel, B&Bs, Food, Drink, Shops, Museum, ATMs, **Gas (petrol) Station &Charging points.**

Assynt Highland Games (37 miles North from Ullapool)

- Held in Early-August each year. Tossing the Caber, Highland dancing, Athletics, and Pipe bands.
  www.assynthighlandgames.com
  Culag Park, Lochinver.

Ullapool to Wick

(175 miles – 4 hr. 40 mins)

Edrachilles Hotel(135 miles to Wick)

- This is an accredited *Scotch Whisky Embassy* with its own qualified Whisky Ambassador and over 100 single malt scotch whiskies in stock.
  www.eddrachilles.com
  A894 2 miles South of Scourie.

Scourie

(133 miles from UllaPool)

- Hotel, B&Bs, Food, Drink, Shops, ATM &**Gas (petrol) Station &Charging points.**

Cocoa Mountain (Shop) (107 miles to Wick)

- Get your chocolate fix here.
  www.cocoamountain.co.uk
  Balnakeil, Durness.

Durness Highland Games

- Held in Late-July each year. Tossing the Caber, Highland dancing, Athletics, and Pipe bands.
  https://secretary134.wixsite.com/highlandgathering
  Shore Park, Durness.

Smoo Cave(105 miles to Wick)

- Visiting the cave is free unless you wish to take a trip further in by boat.
  http://smoocavetours.weebly.com
  Durness.

Durness

(104 miles to Wick)

- B&Bs, Food, Shop, &**Gas (petrol) Station &Charging points.**

Golden Eagle Adventures (100 miles to Wick)

- Zip Lines over the beach (cash only attraction).

Tongue

(75 miles to Wick)

- Hotel, B&Bs, Food, Drink, Post Office, **Gas (petrol) Station &Charging points.**

Bettyhill

(62 miles to Wick)

- Hotel, B&Bs, Food, Drink, Shop, &**Gas (petrol) Station**.

Melvich

(49 miles to Wick)

- **Charging points.**

Wolfburn Distillery(35 Miles to Wick).

- Pronunciation: Wolf-Burn.
- Name Origin: Named for a local burn (stream).
- Established: 2012.
- Location: Henderson Park, Thurso.
- Region: Highland.
- Visitor Center/Tours: Go to website for information.
- Website: https://wolfburn.com
  Henderson Park, Thurso.

Thurso

(34 Miles to Wick)

- Hotel, B&Bs, Food, Drink, Shop, ATMs &**Gas (petrol) Stations &Charging points.**

Halkirk Highland Games(7 miles South of Thurso)

- Held in Late-July each year. Tossing the Caber, Highland dancing, Athletics, and Pipe bands.
  www.halkirkgames.co.uk
  Halkirk Recreation Park, Bridge Street, Halkirk.

Dunnet Bay Distillery(26 Miles to Wick)

- Makers of Rock Rose Gin, North Coast 500 Gin and Holy Grass vodka.

- Tours: Go to website for information.

- www.dunnetbaydistillers.co.uk
  Dunnet, Thurso.

Mey Castle and Gardens(23 Miles to Wick)

- In 1952, HM Queen Elizabeth The Queen Mother purchased the Castle and renovated it.
  www.castleofmey.org.uk

Gills

(16 Miles to Wick)

- **Charging points.**

John O' Groats

(15 Miles to Wick)

Known as the most northerly point in mainland Scotland (it's really Dunnet Head, which is close by).

Castle of Mey Highland Games

- Held in Early-August each year. Tossing the Caber, Highland dancing, Athletics, and Pipe bands.
  www.castleofmey.org.uk
  John O'Groats Showground, The Castle of Mey, Thurso
  .

Wick to Inverness

(103 miles – 2 hrs. 15 mins)

Wick is a good base for exploring the Northern Coast around John O'Groats, or as a stopover for the Orkney ferries.

- Hotels, B&Bs, Food, Drink, Car Hire, Buses, Taxis, Shops, ATMs/Banks, Museum, **Gas (petrol) & Charging Stations**.

Mackays Hotel

- With 165 Whiskies available.
  www.mackayshotel.co.uk
  46 Union Street, Wick.

Old Pulteney Distillery

- Pronunciation: Old Pult-Knee.
- Name Origin: Named for a local area developer.
- Established:1826.
- Location: Huddart Street, Wick.
- Region: Highland.
- Visitor Center/Tours: Go to website for information.
- Website:www.oldpulteney.com

Wick Heritage Museum

- Housing a number of furnished rooms portraying past times. www.wickheritage.org

WhaligoeSteps(97 Miles to Inverness)

- 330 man-made steps down to a natural harbour between the cliffs.

Lybster

(91 Miles to Inverness)

- Hotel, B&Bs, Food, Drink, Shop, ATMs &**Gas (petrol) Stations.**

Helmsdale

(69 Miles to Inverness)

- Hotel, B&Bs, Food, Drink, Shop, ATMs &**Gas (petrol) Stations &Charging points.**

Helmsdale Highland Games (69 Miles to Inverness)

- Held in Mid-August each year. Tossing the Caber, Highland dancing, Athletics, and Pipe bands.
  www.helmsdalegames.co.uk
  Helmsdale.

Clynelish Distillery(59 Miles to Inverness)

- Pronunciation: Cleen-leesh
- Name Origin: Gaelic - "Sloped Garden."
- Established: 1891.
- Location: Clynelish, Brora.
- Region: Highland.
- Visitor Center/Tours: Go to website for information.
- Website:www.malts.com/en-row/distilleries/clynelish

The Sutherland Inn(58 miles to Inverness)

- Has a growing collection of over 220 single malt scotch whiskies and an impressive wine list to compliment the locally sourced and freshly prepared menu.
  www.sutherlandinn.co.uk
  Fountain Square, Brora.

Dunrobin Castle(54 Miles to Inverness)

- The most northerly of Scotland's great houses and one of Britain's oldest continuously inhabited houses dating back to the early 1300s. Home to the Dukes of Sutherland.
  www.dunrobincastle.co.uk
  Golspie, Sutherland.

Golspie

(52 Miles to Inverness)

- Hotel, B&Bs, Food, Drink, Shop, ATMs &**Gas (petrol) Stations.**

Dornoch Castle Hotel (43 miles to Inverness)

- Dating back to the 1400's, the castle also has an on-site distillery. Great Whisky Bar.
  www.dornochcastlehotel.com
  Castle Street, Dornoch.

Dornoch Highland Games (43 miles to Inverness)

- Held in Early-August each year. Tossing the Caber, Highland dancing, Athletics, and Pipe bands.
  www.dornochhighlandgames.org
  The Meadows Park, Dornock.

Cocoa Mountain (Shop)(44 Miles to Inverness)

- Get your chocolate fix here. www.cocoamountain.co.uk

Invercharron Highland Games(39 Miles to Inverness)

- Held in Late-September each year. Tossing the Caber, Highland dancing, Athletics, and Pipe bands.
  www.invercharronhighlandgames.co.uk
  Bonar Bridge.

Glenmorangie Distillery(37 Miles to Inverness)

- Pronunciation: Glen-Mor-an-Gee.
- Name Origin: Gaelic - "Valley of the big meadows."
- Established: 1843.
- Location: Tain, Highlands.
- Region: Highland.
- Visitor Center/Tours: Go to website for information.
- Website:www.glenmorangie.com

Tain

(35 Miles to Inverness)

- Hotel, B&Bs, Food, Drink, Shops, ATMs &**Gas (petrol) Stations &Charging points.**

Tain Highland Gathering

- Held in Mid-July each year. Tossing the Caber, Highland dancing, Athletics, and Pipe bands.
  www.tainhighlandgathering.com
  Glenmorangie Ground, Tain.

Balblair Distillery(6 miles West of Tain)
(4th oldest distillery in Scotland)

- Pronunciation: Bal-blair.
- Name Origin: Gaelic - "The farm on the flat moor."
- Established: 1790.
- Location: Edderton, Tain, Ross-Shire.
- Region: Highland.
- Visitor Center/Tours: Go to website for information.
- Website:www.balblair.com

Mansfield Castle Hotel(34 miles from the City Center)

- Dating back to the Victorian era and nestled in beautiful gardens.
  www.mansfieldcastle.co.uk
  Scotsburn Road, Tain.

Fyrish Monument (25 miles to Inverness)

- Short steep (in parts) climb, great views over the Cromarty Firth.

Kincraig Castle Hotel(24 miles to Inverness)

- Dating from the 1800's and set in 10 acres.
  www.kincraigcastle.co.uk
  Near Tomich on A9 By, Invergordon.

Dalmore Distillery(22 Miles to Inverness)

- Pronunciation: Dal-more
- Name Origin: Gaelic - "The Big Field."
- Established: 1839.
- Location: Alness.
- Region: Highland.
- Visitor Center/Tours: Go to website for information.
- Website:www.thedalmore.com

Teaninich Distillery (22 Miles to Inverness)

- Pronunciation: Tea-na-nik
- Name Origin: Gaelic - "The house on the moor."
- Established: 1817.
- Location: Riverside Drive, Alness.
- Region: Highland.
- Visitor Center/Tours: Go to website for information.
- Websitehttps://scotchwhisky.com/whiskypedia/1899/teaninich

Castle Leod(19 miles to Inverness)

- The Seat of Clan Mackenzie (the Earl of Cromartie) for over 500 years.
www.castleleod.org.uk
Strathpeffer.

Strathpeffer Highland Games (19 miles to Inverness)

- Held in Early-August each year. Tossing the Caber, Highland dancing, Athletics, and Pipe bands. www.strathpefferhighlandgathering.com *Castle Leod, Strathpeffer.*

Tulloch Castle Hotel(16 miles from the City Center)

- Dating back to the 1100's, with a 250-year-old Great Hall and wonderful ceilings. www.bespokehotels.com/tullochcastlehotel *Tulloch Castle Drive, Dingwall.*

The Black Isle Brewery(8 miles to Inverness)

- Making Craft beers since 1998.
- Location: Munlochy.
- Tours: Go to website for information.
- Price: Free, but tours only last 15 minutes.
- Website:www.blackislebrewery.com

Chapter 8

Orkney and Shetland

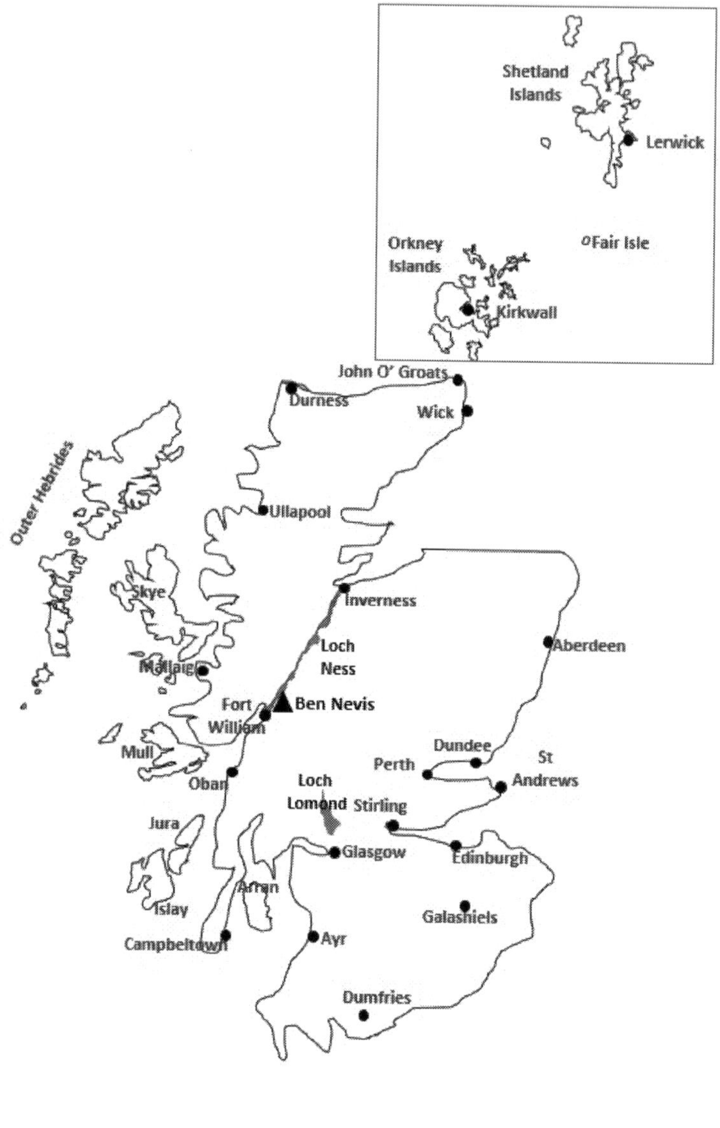

Orkney(Pop. 22,000)

20 miles across the Pentland Firth at the top of mainland Scotland lie the Orkney islands.
Consisting of 70 islands, 20 of them inhabited.
You can either arrive by Ferry or fly into Orkney. I did neither, I went on a Navy ship (but, that's probably not an option).
The remote locations, small populations and lack of light pollution on these islands make for great star gazing and viewing the northern lights (best in winter).
There is ample opportunity to walk/hike or bike and see the beautiful scenery, view the wildlife and work up an appetite for some incredible seafood.
I am assuming a start point of Kirkwall as it is the main town and ferry port of the isle.
Beautiful scenery, lots of wildlife and incredible seafood are all available here.

Getting there, Kirkwall Airport;

From

- Aberdeen, Bergen (Norway), Edinburgh, Fair Isle, Glasgow, Inverness, and Sumburg.
  www.hial.co.uk/kirkwall-airport

By Ferry

Northlink

- From Scrabster, Mainland to Stromness, Orkney.
- From Aberdeen, Mainland to Kirkwall, Orkney.

  www.northlinkferries.co.uk

Pentland

- From Gill's Bay, Mainland to St Margret's Hope, South Ronaldsay, Orkney.
- From St Margret's Hope, South Ronaldsay, Orkney to Kirkwall, Orkney.

  www.pentlandferries.co.uk

Orkney Folk Festival

- With local Orcadian and international artists this 4-day festival is held late-May each year. www.orkneyfolkfestival.com

St Magnus Festival

- Orkney's celebration of the arts held annually in mid-June, with venues all over Orkney. www.stmagnusfestival.com

Kirkwall (Pop. 9,500)

Since 1486 Kirkwall has been a Royal Burgh and the main town and port.

- Hotels, B&Bs, Food, Drink, Buses, Taxis, Car Hire, Shops, ATMs/Banks, Post Office, **Gas (petrol)& Charging Stations**.

Bishop and Earls Palace

- Built in the 1100s around the same time as St Magnus Cathedral. It was remodeled in the early 1600s into a renaissance palace. Now a ruin, but well worth a visit. www.orkney.com

Highland Park Distillery

- Pronunciation: Highland-Park
- Name Origin: 'Highland' refers to the location of the distillery and 'Park' is the Orcadian name for farmland.
- Established: 1798.
- Location: Holm road, Kirkwall.
- Region: Island.
- Visitor Center/Tours: Go to website for information.
- www.highlandparkwhisky.com

Orkney Distilling Company

- Making Gin. Tours and tastings available, go to website for information. www.orkneydistilling.com

Orkney Museum

- Orkney's story starts in the Stone Age, and journeys through the Picts and Vikings, right up to the present day. www.orkney.gov.uk

Scapa Distillery

- Pronunciation: Scap-A
- Name Origin: Old Norse - "Boat."
- Established: 1885.
- Location: Scapa, Kirkwall.
- Region: Island.
- Visitor Center/Tours: Go to website for information.
- www.scapawhisky.com

St Magnus Cathedral

- "The light in the North." Founded in 1137 by the Viking, Earl Rognvald, in honour of his uncle St Magnus who was martyred in Orkney. www.stmagnus.org

St Magnus Festival

- Orkney's celebration of the arts held annually in mid-June, with venues all over Orkney. www.stmagnusfestival.com

Italian Chapel (8 miles from Kirkwall)

- Small, but beautiful chapel built during the second World War by Italian prisoners of war. www.orkney.com

Maeshowe (10 miles from Kirkwall)

- Prehistoric chambered cairn dating from around 2700BC. www.orkneyjar.com

Standing Stones of Stenness (10 miles from Kirkwall)

- Henge monument around 5,000-years-old. One mile from the Ring of Brodgar. www.historicenvironment.scot

Ness of Brodgar(10.5 miles from Kirkwall)

- A large complex of Neolithic buildings. Halfway between the Standing Stones of Stenness and the Ring of Brodgar. www.nessofbrodgar.co.uk

Ring of Brodgar (11 miles from Kirkwall)

- Massive stone circle and many burial mounds. One mile from the Standing Stones of Stenness.
  www.historicenvironment.scot

Deerness Distillery (12 miles from Kirkwall)

- Making Gin and Vodka. Tours and tastings available, go to website for information.
  www.deernessdistillery.com

Aikerness (16 miles from Kirkwall)

- Broch of Gurness Iron Age village, approx. 2,000-years-old
  www.historicenvironment.scot

Orkney Brewery (18 miles from Kirkwall)

- Tours and tastings available, booking advised. Information on their website.
  www.orkneybrewery.co.uk

Stromness

(19 miles from Kirkwall)

The second largest town in the Orkneys.

- Hotels, B&Bs, Food, Drink, Buses, Taxis, Shops, ATMs, Post Office, **Gas (petrol) & Charging Stations**.

By Ferry

Stromness Terminal (15 miles from Kirkwall)

- From Stromness, Mainland to Graemsay/Hoy. www.orkneyferries.co.uk

- **Oktoberfest** – Fire, Meat& Ale. Held annually in late October. Beer, Traditional music, Viking feast, Viking games, Fire procession (open to the public) and galley burning. www.orkney.com/events/orktoberfest-fire-maet-ale

Skara Brae (19 miles from Kirkwall)

- Neolithic village inhabited for around 600 years, between 3200BC and 2200BC. Re-discovered in 1850 after a huge storm unearthed it. www.orkneyjar.com/history/skarabrae

Orkney Brewery (22 miles from Kirkwall)

- Tours and tastings available, booking advised. Information on their website. www.orkneybrewery.co.uk

Isle of Hoy(26 miles from Kirkwall by road and Ferry)

- The second largest island in the Orkney group has the UK's tallest sea stack at 450ft high, the "Old Man of Hoy." This stunning rock pillar can be seen from describer to Stromness ferry.

Shetland(Pop. 23,000)

110 miles north from the mainland of Scotland and around 50 miles north/east of the Orkney islands lie the Shetland islands. Consisting of around 100 islands, 17 of them inhabited.
You can either arrive by Ferry or fly into Shetland. I arrived on a Navy ship and flew out from Sumburg airport (25 miles from Lerwick). I am assuming a start point of Lerwick as it is the main town and ferry port of the isle. There is ample opportunity to walk/hike or bike and see the beautiful scenery, view the wildlife and work up an appetite for some incredible seafood.

By Air to Sumburg Airport
From

- Aberdeen, Bergen (Norway), Edinburgh, Glasgow, Inverness, and Kirkwall.
  www.hial.co.uk/sumburgh-airport

By Ferry

Northlink Terminal (1 mile from Lerwick)

- From Scrabster, Mainland to Stromness, Shetland.
- From Aberdeen, Mainland to Kirkwall.

www.northlinkferries.co.uk

Lerwick(Pop. 7,000)

The main town and port.

- Hotels, B&Bs, Food, Drink, Car Hire, Shops, ATMs/Banks, Post Office, **Gas (petrol)& Charging Stations**.

Shetland Folk Festival

- Various venues throughout Shetland. Held late April, early May each year. www.shetlandfolkfestival.com

Up Helly Aa

- A series of fire festivals held throughout the island from January to March each year, with the main one held on the last Tuesday of January in Lerwick. www.uphellyaa.org

Lerwick Brewery(2 miles from Lerwick)

- Tours and tastings available, booking advised. Information on their website. www.lerwickbrewery.co.uk

Old Scatness Broch & Iron Age Village
(23 miles from Lerwick)

- Iron age Broch (stone tower) and village. 3 miles from Jarlshof. www.shetlandamenity.org/old-scatness

Jarlshof Prehistoric & Norse Settlement
(26 miles from Lerwick)

- This site contains remains dating from 2500 BC up to the 17th century AD. Covering the Bronze age, Iron age, Pictish age and the Viking age.3 miles from Old Scatness Broch & Iron Age Village. www.historicenvironment.scot

Tangwick Haa Museum (38 miles from Lerwick)

- The museum is situated within a restored 17th-century house. www.tangwickhaa.org.uk

Chapter 9

Stay in a Castle or Stately Home.

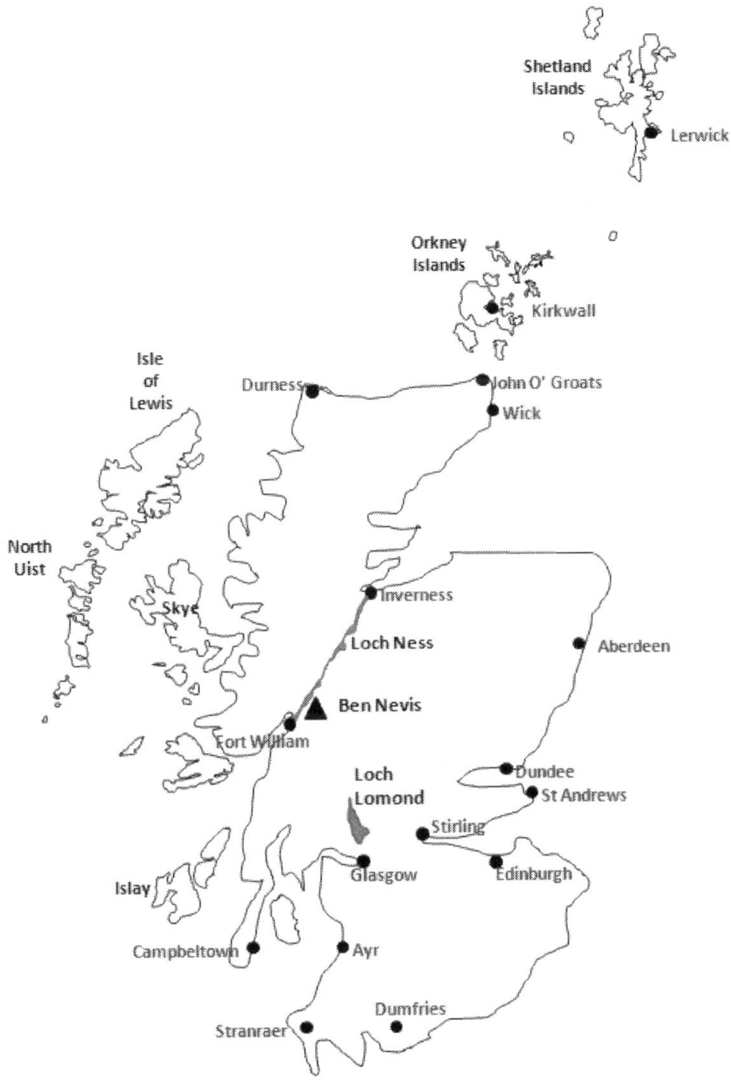

Near Aberdeen

Ardoe House(7 miles from the City Center)

- 19th-century mansion house set in 30 acres.
  https://all.accor.com/hotel/6626/index.en.shtml
  Aberdeen.

Macleod House & Lodge (11 miles from the City Center)

- Historic mansion house which has been extensively renovated to make it into a 19-bedroom luxury hotel.
  www.trumphotels.com
  Aberdeen.

Leslie Castle Hotel(29 miles North West from theCity Center)

- Built in 1661, Leslie Castle now offers delightful adults only, B&B. Delicious Scottish breakfasts are cooked to order, dinner can be provided if you book in advance.
  https://leslie-castle.com
  Leslie, Insch.

Near Ayr

Culzean CastleHotel(13 miles from the town center)

- This Castle sits in the heart of Burns country, making a great base for visiting the poet's haunts.
  www.culzean-eisenhower.com
  Maybole.

Braemar

Fife Arms Hotel

- Victorian coaching inn built in the 19th century.
  https://thefifearms.com
  Mar Road, Braemar, Ballater.

Near Dumfries

SpringkellHotel(21 miles from the town center)

- Mansion house dating from 1734, located close to the historic town of Gretna Green. Individual rooms can now be booked on a dinner, bed and breakfast basis.
  www.springkell.com
  Lockerbie.

Near Edinburgh

Balmoral hotel

- Sitting at the junction of Princes street and the bridge up to the Royal Mile. This luxury five-star hotel which was built in 1902, is an Edinburgh landmark. Their Whisky bar appropriately named "Scotch" has over 500 whiskies on offer.
  www.roccofortehotels.com
  1 Princes street.

Barony Castle HouseHotel(19 miles from the City Center)

- 16th century mansion house, featuring an indoor heated swimming pool.
  www.baronycastle.com
  Eddleston, Scottish Borders.

Carberry TowerHotel(10 miles from the City Center)

- Hotel with a history dating back to the 1400s.
  https://carberrytower.com
  Carberry Tower Estate, Musselburgh.

Cornhill CastleHotel(32 miles from the City Center)

- Built in the French Renaissance style, this stately building sits beside the River Clyde. Offering locally sourced food in the Ghillie Restaurant.
  www.cornhillcastle.co.uk
  Coulter Road, Biggar.

CringletieHotel(20 miles from the City Center)

- Scottish Baronial home with fine dining in the Sutherland Restaurant.
  www.cringletie.com
  Edinburgh Road, Peebles.

Dalhousie Castle Hotel(10 miles from the City Center)

- 13th century castle with dining in a vaulted dungeon.
  www.dalhousiecastle.co.uk
  Cockpen Road, Bonnyrigg.

Fa'side Castle Hotel(10 miles from the City Center)

- B&B accommodation situated at the top of the 14th century tower.
  www.faside-estate.com
  Tranent.

Fenton Tower(25 miles East from the City Center)

- Fortified 16th Century tower.
  www.fentontower.com
  North Berwick.

Melville CastleHotel(8 miles from the City Center)

- Family run hotel located on the outskirts of Edinburgh. Offering charming accommodation, an atmospheric restaurant.
  https://melvillecastle.com
  Gilmerton Road, Lasswade.

Scotsman hotel

- Taking its name from the national newspaper that used to inhabit the building (Built in 1905), this luxury hotel has stunning views across Edinburgh.
  https://scotsmanhotel.co.uk
  20 North Bridge, Edinburgh.

Shieldhill Castle Hotel(29 miles from the City Center)

- The Castle was opened in 1199 and renovated in 2012.
  https://shieldhill-castle-hotel-biggar.hotelmix.co.uk
  Shieldhill Road, Quothquan, Biggar.

Thirlestane CastleHotel(28 miles from the town center)

- Built originally as a defensive fort in the 13th century, it was re-built in the 16th century as a home.
  www.thirlestanecastle.co.uk
  Lauder.

Traquair CastleHotel(29 miles from the City Center)

- Scotland's oldest inhabited house dating back to 1107. Originally owned by the kings of Scotland, as a hunting lodge. Subsequently the home of the Earls of Traquair. Visited by 27 Kings and Queens including Mary Queen of Scots.
  https://www.traquair.co.uk
  Traquair, Innerleithen.

Near Falkirk

Powfoulis House Hotel (26 miles East from George Square)

- Country Manor house, that was in the hands of the Bruce family for 10 generations.
  www.powfoulis.com
  Bothkennar, Falkirk

Near Fort William

Glengarry Castle Hotel(24 miles from the town center)

- This 19th century country house sits in 60 acres on Loch Oich.
  www.glengarry.net
  Glengarry.

Inverlochy CastleHotel(3 miles from the town center)

- This 19th century castle sits amongst the foothills of Scotland's highest mountain - the mighty Ben Nevis.
  https://inverlochycastlehotel.com
  Torlundy, Fort William.

Mingary Castle Hotel(67 miles from the town center)

- This 13th century Castle stands atop a rocky outcrop above the Sound of Mull.
  www.ardnamurchanestate.co.uk/blog/mingary-castle
  Arisaig.

The InchHotel(33 miles from Fort William)

- Inchnacardoch theformer hunting lodge of Lord Lovat on the shores of Loch Ness.
  https://inchhotel.com
  Fort Augustus, Inverness-shire.

NearGlasgow

Sherbrooke Castle Hotel(4 miles from George Square)

- Lovely Baronial House built in 1896, with restaurant and bar.
  https://sherbrookecastlehotel.com
  11 Sherbrooke Avenue, Bellahouston.

Crossbasket Castle Hotel(8 miles from George Square)

- This 17th century castle has been transformed into one of Scotland's most luxurious hotels.
  www.crossbasketcastle.com
  Stoneymeadow Road, East Kilbride.

Cameron House Hotel (25 miles from George Square)

- Baronial Mansion sitting on the "Bonnie, Bonnie banks" of Loch Lomond.
  www.cameronhouse.co.uk
  Alexandria, Loch Lomond.

Castle LevanHotel(32 miles from George Square)

- Castle Levan was built circa 1457. B&B accommodation in 2 guest bedchambers.
  www.castle-levan.com
  Gourock.

Near Inverness

Bunchrew House Hotel(4 miles from the City Center) (**NC500**)

- Dating back to 1641 this Scottish mansion sits in beautiful gardens on the shores of the Beauly Firth.
  https://bunchrewhousehotel.com
  Bunchrew.

Dornoch Castle Hotel(43 miles from the City Center) (**NC500**)

- Dating back to the 1400's, the castle also has an on-site distillery. Great Whisky Bar.
  www.dornochcastlehotel.com
  Castle Street, Dornoch.

Kincraig Castle Hotel(23 miles from the City Center) (**NC500**)

- Dating from the 1800's and set in 10 acres.
  www.kincraigcastle.co.uk
  Near Tomich on A9 By, Invergordon.

Mansfield Castle Hotel(34 miles from the City Center) (**NC500**)

- Dating back to the Victorian era and nestled in beautiful gardens.
  www.mansfieldcastle.co.uk
  Scotsburn Road, Tain.

Tulloch Castle Hotel(16 miles from the City Center) (**NC500**)

- Dating back to the 1100's, with a 250-year-old Great Hall and wonderful ceilings.
  www.bespokehotels.com/tullochcastlehotel
  Tulloch Castle Drive, Dingwall.

Near Kelso

Duns Castle Hotel(16 miles from Kelso)

- 14th century castle.
  https://dunscastle.co.uk
  Duns.

Near Kilmarnock

Craufurdland Castle Hotel (4 miles North from Kilmarnock)

- Built in the 13th-century and set in a beautiful estate.
  https://craufurdland.co.uk
  Craufurdland Castle, Kilmarnock.

Near Melrose

Abbottsford House & Hotel(38 miles South from the Scott Monument, Edinburgh)

- Abbottsford house, home to Sir Walter Scott.
  www.scottsabbotsford.com
  Abbotsford House, Melrose.

Near Oban

Barcaldine Castle Hotel(10 miles from the town center)

- 17th century tower house castle with breakfast accommodation.
  www.barcaldinecastle.co.uk
  Benderloch.

Lunga House Hotel (23 Miles South from Oban)

- 16th Century Tower House.
  www.lungahouse.co.uk
  Craob haven.

Kilmartin Castle Hotel(29 miles from the town center)

- This 500-year-old Castle is now a luxury bed and breakfast venue.
  www.kilmartincastle.com
  Kilmartin, Lochgilphead.

Near Peebles

Neidpath Castle Hotel(1-mile West from Peebles)

- Stay in a 16th Century Castle.
  www.neidpathcastle.com
  Neidpath Castle, Peebles.

Near Perth

Atholl Palace Hotel(27 miles from the City Center)

- Set in 48 acres of gardens/woodland, with swimming pool, Spa, restaurant and whisky bar.
  www.athollpalace.com
  Perth Road, Pitlochry.

Dalmunzie CastleHotel(36 miles from the City Center)

- An elegant country house hotel.
  www.dalmunzie.com
  Spittal of Glenshee, Blairgowrie.

Fonab CastleHotel(27 miles from the City Center)

- The hotel offers a choice of two restaurants and a cellar with a fine selection of wines, whiskies and gins.
  www.fonabcastlehotel.com
  Foss Road, Pitlochry.

Knock Castle Hotel(18 miles from the City Center)

- Built in the 1800's as a stately home.
  www.knockcastle.com
  40 Drummond Terrace, Crieff.

Near Portree(Isle of Skye)

Kinloch LodgeHotel(33 miles from Portree)

- Lord Macdonald's former hunting lodge on the shores of Loch Na Dal.
  https://kinloch-lodge.co.uk
  Sleat, Isle of Skye.

Skeabost Lodge

- A 19th century hunting lodge, built in 1871.
  www.skeabosthotel.com
  Portree.

Near Selkirk

Aikwood Tower Hotel(5 miles West from Selkirk)

- Tower House hotel. The first mention of Aikwood comes in the Lord Treasurer of Scotland's accounts of 1455.
  www.aikwoodtower.com
  Aikwood Tower, Selkirk.

Near St Andrews

Fernie Castle(15 miles from St Andrews)

- First established in 1353, the present castle dates back almost 500 years.
  http://ferniecastle.co.uk
  Cupar.

Myers Castle (19 miles from St Andrews)

- This almost 500-year-old Castle built in 1530 is nestled in the Kingdom of Fife.
  www.myrescastle.co.uk
  Cupar.

Near Stirling

Airth Castle(10 miles from Stirling Castle)

- Once owned by the family of Robert the Bruce and dating back to the 14th century.
  www.airthcastlehotel.com
  Airth.

Broomhall Castle Hotel(6 miles from Stirling Castle)

- Built in 1836 in the style of Balmoral castle. With views of Stirling Castle and the Wallace Monument.
  www.broomhallcastle.co.uk
  Long Row, Menstrie.

Near Stornoway

Lews Castle & Museum

- Built in 1847 and now home to the famous Lewis chessmen. Offering self-catering and hotel rooms.
  www.lews-castle.co.uk
  Stornoway.

Near Stranraer

Glenapp Castle Hotel(15 miles from the town center)

- Welcome to Glenapp Castle, an award winning 5-star Castle Hotel.
  www.glenappcastle.com
  Ballantrae, Girvan.

North West Castle Hotel(0.5 miles from the town center)

- North West Castle was built in 1820 on the shores of Loch Ryan.
  www.mcmillanhotels.co.uk/hotels/north-west-castle
  Port Rodie, Stranraer.

Near Tarbert(Isle of Harris)

Amhuinnsuidhe Castle Hotel(6 miles from the town center)

- Built in 1865 in the Scottish Baronial style. http://amhuinnsuidhe-com.stackstaging.com *Amhuinnsuidh.*

Stonefield Castle Hotel(2 miles from Tarbert)

- Scottish baronial styled castle dating back to 1837. www.bespokehotels.com/stonefieldcastle *Stonefield, Tarbert.*

Near Tobermory(Isle of Mull)

Glengorm Castle Hotel(5 miles from the town center)

- Dating from 1860, in the Scottish Baronial style. www.glengormcastle.co.uk *Glengorm Castle, Tobermory.*

Chapter 10

Long Distance Hiking Trails

For a full interactive map and a wealth of information on hiking in Scotland go to www.walkhighlands.co.uk
What follows is meant to whet your appetite for more hikes and point you to more comprehensive information.

Affric Kintail Way

From Drumnadrochit to Morvich in Kintail.
Distance: 44mi/71km
Duration: 5-10 days
Height Gain: 2640ft/ 800m
www.affrickintailway.com

Annandale Way

From the mouth of the River Annan and Solway Firth to Annandale Head in the hills north of the town of Moffat.
Distance: 55mi/ 88km
Duration: 5 days
Height Gain: 3780ft/ 1152m
http://annandaleway.org

Arran Coastal Way

A circuit around the isle of Arran.
Distance: 66mi/109km
Duration: 10 days
Height Gain: 6863ft/2092m*
*This is dependent on whether you take in Goatfell mountain or any of the alternate routes or not.
www.coastalway.co.uk

Ayrshire Coastal Path

Follows the coastline for most of the hike with great views.
Distance: 100mi/150km
Duration: 5-10 days
Height Gain: 2640ft/800m
http://ayrshirecoastalpath.org

Berwickshire Coastal Path

As the name suggests, this trail follows the coast.
Distance: 30mi/48km
Duration: 2-4 days
Height Gain: 3280ft/1000m
https://walkscottishborders.com/route/berwickshire-coastal-path

Borders Abbeys Way

A circular hike connecting the historic Border towns and their famous Abbeys.
Distance: 64.4mi/103km
Duration: 4 days
Height Gain: 990ft/300m
www.bordersabbeysway.com

Cape Wrath Trail

The Cape Wrath Trail is a long-distance walk from Fort William to the north western most point of mainland Britain, Cape Wrath. This is one for experienced hikers only, you will need to be competent with a map and compass, as the way is unmarked. you will also need to carry a tent and supplies for most of the way, you will be traversing rough ground and fording rivers. This is not a hike to do on a whim.

Distance: 235mi/378km
Duration: 14 to 18 days
Height Gain: 33543ft/10224m
https://capewrathtrailguide.org

Clyde Walkway

Distance: 40mi/65km
Duration: 5 days
Height Gain: 2355ft/718m
www.walkhighlands.co.uk

Cateran Trail

Named after local cattle rustlers, is a circular route from Blairgowrie.

Distance: 60mi/96km
Duration: 5 days
Height Gain: 3168ft/960m
www.walkthecaterantrail.com

Cowal Way

Takes you through Argyll's Cowal peninsula running from Portavadie to Ardgartan.
Distance: 57mi/92km
Duration: 5 days
Height Gain: 5082ft/1540m
www.cowalway.co.uk

Dava Way

Looking at the distance, not that hard, but there is only accommodation at either end, so you will need to take a tent and supplies with you.
Distance: 23mi/38km
Duration: 1 to 3 days
Height Gain: 480ft/146m
www.walkhighlands.co.uk

East Highland Way

Partly way marked, partly wild hiking.
Distance: 80mi/128km
Duration: 4 to 7 days
Height Gain: 4622ft/1409m
www.easthighlandway.com

Fife Coastal Path

A relatively easy hike, with views over the river Forth to Edinburgh and the bridges.
Distance: 117mi/188km
Duration: 7 - 9 days
Height Gain: 330ft/100m
www.fifecoastalpath.co.uk

Formartine and Buchan Way

Aberdeen to Peterhead and Fraserburgh or vice-versa along an old railway.
Distance: 53mi/86km
Duration: 5 days
Height Gain: 660ft/200m
www.walkhighlands.co.uk

Forth & Clyde and Union Canals

Walking on towpaths, easy access to hotels, food and transport.
Distance: 63mi/101km
Duration: 3 to 4 days
Height Gain: 654ft/188m
www.walkhighlands.co.uk

John Muir Way

Coast to coast, crossing Scotland's heartland from Dunbar in the East to Helensburgh in the West
Distance: 134mi/215 km
Duration: 7-10 days
Height Gain: 330ft/100m
Yes, there is a John Muir way in Scotland as well as America, this is the route that he walked from his home in Dunbar across Scotland to Helensburgh to catch the boat to America. This route passes through the area I grew up in, some lovely coastal walks and castles to visit.
http://johnmuirway.org

John O'Groats Trail

This is not a formal trail, so there is little, to no way marking.

Distance: 146mi/235km
Duration: 14 days
Height Gain: 15206ft/4635m
www.walkhighlands.co.uk

Kelvin Way

Glasgow to Milngavie, although not a long-distance path, you can start with this and join onto the West Highland Way at Milngavie. The Kelvin way runs from the center of Glasgow, to Milngavie. The route mainly follows three rivers the Allander, Kelvin and Clyde.

Distance: 11 mi/17km
Duration: 5 hours
Height Gain: 548ft/167m
www.walkhighlands.co.uk

Kintyre Way

Traversing the Kintyre penninsuala.

Distance: 88mi/142km
Duration: 4-7 days
Height Gain: 1320ft/400m
I highly recommend staying at the Ardshiel hotel in Campbeltown (https://ardshiel.co.uk) if you hike this route. The food is superb, the whisky selection is huge (over 700).
www.kintyreway.com

Minigaig Pass

Recommended for experienced hikers only. From Blair Atholl to Kingussie.

Distance: 27mi/42km
Duration: 1-2 days
Height Gain: 3696ft/1120m
www.ldwa.org.uk

Moray Coast Trail

Paths and sandy beaches.

Distance: 45mi/72km
Duration: 3 to 5 days
Height Gain: 1345ft/410m
www.morayways.org.uk/moray-coast-trail.asp

Mull of Galloway Trail

Paths and sandy beaches.

Distance: 45mi/72km
Duration: 3 days
Height Gain: 1345ft/410m
www.walkhighlands.co.uk

RiverAyr Way

Glenbuck in East Ayrshire to the town of Ayr.

Distance: 41mi/66km
Duration: 2 to 4 days
Height Gain: 1540ft/469m
www.walkhighlands.co.uk

Rob Roy Way

The Rob Roy Way joins the town of Drymen to the Highland Perthshire town of Pitlochry.

Distance: 93mi/148km
Duration: 7 days
Height Gain: 1650ft/500m
www.robroyway.com

Scottish National Trail

Scotland's longest route, crossing Scotland from South to North or vice versa.

Extract from the walk Highlands website;
"The Scottish National Trail is a challenging, 864-kilometre-long unofficial long-distance walking route running the length of Scotland from Kirk Yetholm to Cape Wrath.
The route combines sections of official routes such as St Cuthbert's Way, the Southern Upland Way, the Forth and Clyde and Union Canals, the West Highland Way and the Rob Roy Way. Other parts - including sections through central Perthshire, the Cairngorms and the Northwest Highlands - make for a more serious backpacking route with neither way marking nor a continuous path, as well as a number of potentially hazardous river crossings."
Go to their website below for all the details.
Distance: 536mi/864km
Duration: 35 days
Height Gain: If you are willing to try this, then who cares about the height gain.
www.walkhighlands.co.uk

Skye Trail

Challenging, unofficial route for experienced hikers.
Distance: 80mi/128km
Duration: 7 days
Height Gain: 12404ft/3781m
www.walkhighlands.co.uk

Southern Upland Way

Used to be Scotland's longest route, crossing Scotland from coast-to-coast, until the National Trail (above) came along.
Distance: 212mi/340km
Duration: 12-20 days
Height Gain: 4785ft/1450m
www.southernuplandway.gov.uk

South Loch Ness Trail

From Fort Augustus to Inverness using the South side of the loch.
Distance: 36mi/58km
Duration: 3 days
Height Gain: 4461ft/1360m
www.walkhighlands.co.uk

Speyside Way

From Buckie on the Moray Coast to Aviemore in the Cairngorms, because it's easier walking down hill (South).
Distance: 65mi/105km
Duration: 4-7 days
Height Gain: 1650ft/500m
www.speysideway.org

St Cuthbert's Way

Connecting the Scottish border town of Melrose (and it's Abbey) with the holy island of Lindisfarne in England.
Distance: 62mi/100km
Duration: 4 days
Height Gain: 221ft/370m
www.stcuthbertsway.info

The Great Glen Way

Walking alongside lochs and through forests.
Distance: 79mi/127km
Duration: 5 to 7 days
Height Gain: 7253ft/2211m
www.highland.gov.uk/ggw

The West Highland Way

The West Highland Way was Scotland's first long distance route and is still the most popular. Stretching for 95 miles from Milngavie (Mulguy) on the edge of Glasgow to Fort William in the highlands.
Distance: 95mi/153km
Duration: 6 days
Height Gain: 9016ft/2748m
www.westhighlandway.org

The West Island Way

This route takes you across the island of Bute.
Distance: 27mi/45km
Duration: 2 to 3 days
Height Gain: 3064ft/934m
www.walkhighlands.co.uk

Three Lochs Way

This way links Loch Lomond, Gare Loch and Loch Long.
Distance: 33mi/53km
Duration: 3 to 4 days
Height Gain: 3845ft/1172m
www.walkhighlands.co.uk

Chapter 11

Highland Games and Gatherings.

May

Blackford Highland Games (25 miles North from Dunfermline Abbey)

- Held Late-May each year. Tossing the Caber, Highland dancing, Athletics, and Pipe bands. http://blackfordhighlandgames.co.uk Blackford, Auchterarder.

Carmunnock Highland Games (8 miles South from George Square)

- Held Late-May each year. Tossing the Caber, Highland dancing, Athletics, and Pipe bands. http://blackfordhighlandgames.co.uk Carmunnock, Glasgow.

Gordon Castle Highland Games (11 miles East from Elgin)

- Held Mid-May each year at the castle. Tossing the Caber, Highland dancing, Athletics, and Pipe bands.
  www.gordoncastle.co.uk/highland-games
  Gordon Castle Gordon Castle Estate, Fochabers.

Gourock Highland Games

- Held early-May each year at Battery Park. Tossing the Caber, Highland dancing, Athletics, and Pipe bands.
  www.inverclyde.gov.uk
  Battery Park Sports Pavilion, Eldon Street, Greenock.

June

Ardrossan Highland Games

- Held in early-June each year. Tossing the Caber, Highland dancing, Athletics, and Pipe bands.
  www.ardrossanhighlandgames.org.uk
  Memorial Field Pavilion, Sorbie Road, Ardrossan.

Bearsden and Milngavie Highland Games
(7 miles North from George Square)

- Held in early-June each year. Tossing the Caber, Highland dancing, Athletics, and Pipe bands.
  www.bearsdenmilngaviehighlandgames.com
  Burnbrae the Home of West Rugby, Glasgow Rodd, Milngavie.

Carrick Lowland Gathering (22 miles South from Ayr)

- Held in early-June each year. Tossing the Caber, Highland dancing, Athletics, and Pipe bands.
  www.girvanattractions.co.uk/lowland-gathering.php
  Victory Park, Girvan.

Ceres Highland Games (Free)
(30 miles East from Dunfermline Abbey)

- Held in Late-June each year. Tossing the Caber, Highland dancing, Athletics, and Pipe bands.
  www.ceresgames.co.uk
  St Andrews Road, Ceres, Cupar.

Cornhill Highland Games (43 miles West from Peterhead)

- Held early-June each year. Tossing the Caber, Highland dancing, Athletics, and Pipe bands. www.shottshighlandgames.org.uk
Cornhill Playing Field, Banff.

Cupar Highland Games (30 miles East from Dunfermline Abbey)

- Held in Mid-June each year. Tossing the Caber, Highland dancing, Athletics, and Pipe bands.
http://cuparhighlandgames.org
41 Carslogie Road, Cupar.

Drumtochty Highland Games (13 miles West from Stonehaven)

- Held at the castle in Late-June each year. Tossing the Caber, Highland dancing, Athletics, and Pipe bands.
www.spanglefish.com/drumtochtyhighlandgames
Laurencekirk.

Gairloch Highland Gathering (23 miles West from Kinlochewe)

- Held in Late-June/early July each year. Tossing the Caber, Highland dancing, Athletics, and Pipe bands.
  www.shottshighlandgames.org.uk
  Sands Caravan & Camping Gairloch, Wester Ross.

Helensburgh and Lomond Highland Games

- Held early-June each year. Tossing the Caber, Highland dancing, Athletics, and Pipe bands.
  www.helensburghandlomondgames.co.uk
  Rugby Ground, Helensburgh.

Lorne Highland Games

- Held in Late-June each year. Tossing the Caber, Highland dancing, Athletics, and Pipe bands.
  http://lorne-highland-games.org.uk
  Oban.

Markinch Highland Games (20 miles East from Dunfermline Abbey)

- Held in early-June each year. Tossing the Caber, Highland dancing, Athletics, and Pipe bands.
  www.shottshighlandgames.org.uk
  John Dixon Park, Markinch, Glenrothes.

Old Meldrum Sports and Highland Games (18 miles North from Aberdeen)

- Held in Mid-June each year. Tossing the Caber, Highland dancing, Athletics, and Pipe bands.
  www.oldmeldrumsports.co.uk
  Park Cresent, Oldmeldrum, Inverurie.

Shotts Highland Games (24 miles East from George Square)

- Held early-June each year. Tossing the Caber, Highland dancing, Athletics, and Pipe bands.
  www.shottshighlandgames.org.uk
  Hannah Park, Shotts.

Strathmore Highland Games (7 miles West of Forfar)

- Held at Glamis Castle in early-June each year. Tossing the Caber, Highland dancing, Athletics, and Pipe bands.
  www.shottshighlandgames.org.uk
  Glamis Castle, Forfar.

July

Airth Highland Games **(9 miles East and South from Stirling Castle)**

- Held in Late-July each year. Tossing the Caber, Highland dancing, Athletics, and Pipe bands.
  www.airthgames.co.uk
  Airth.

Alva Highland Games (7 miles North from Stirling Castle)

- Held in Mid-July each year. Tossing the Caber, Highland dancing, Athletics, and Pipe bands.
  http://alva.ukctest.co.uk
  Johnstone Park, Alva.

Arisaig Highland Games & Clan Donald Gathering (36 miles North/West from Fort William)

- Held in Late-July each year. Tossing the Caber, Highland dancing, Athletics, and Pipe bands.
  www.arisaighighlandgames.co.uk
  Arisaig.

Balquhidder, Lochearnhead & Strathyre Highland Games (37 miles West from Perth)

- Held in Late-July each year. Tossing the Caber, Highland dancing, Athletics, and Pipe bands.
  http://lochearnheadhighlandgames.co.uk
  Lochearnhead.

Braemar Junior Highland Games

- Junior Highland games held in Braemar in Mid-July. Tossing the Caber, Highland dancing, Athletics, and Pipe bands.
  www.braemarjuniorgames.com
  Princess Royal and Duke of Fife Memorial Park, Braemar.

Burntisland Highland Games (11 miles East from Dunfermline Abbey)

- Held in Late-July each year. Tossing the Caber, Highland dancing, Athletics, and Pipe bands.
  https://burntislandhighlandgames.co.uk
  Burntisland Links, Kinghorn Road, Burntisland.

City of Inverness Highland Games

- Held in Late-July each year. Tossing the Caber, Highland dancing, Athletics, and Pipe bands.
  http://invernesshighlandgames.com
  Bught Park, Inverness.

Dufftown Highland Games (17 miles South from Elgin)

- Held in Late-July each year. Tossing the Caber, Highland dancing, Athletics, and Pipe bands.
  www.dufftownhighlandgames.com
  Mortlach Community Field, Hill Street, Dufftown.

Durness Highland Games

- Held in Late-July each year. Tossing the Caber, Highland dancing, Athletics, and Pipe bands.
  https://secretary134.wixsite.com/highlandgathering
  Shore Park, Durness.

Forres Highland Games (12 miles West from Elgin)

- Held in Early-July each year. Tossing the Caber, Highland dancing, Athletics, and Pipe bands.
  www.forreshighlandgames.com
  2002 Clovenside Road, Forres.

Gairloch Highland Gathering (23 miles West from Kinlochewe)

- Held in Late-June/early July each year. Tossing the Caber, Highland dancing, Athletics, and Pipe bands.
  www.shottshighlandgames.org.uk
  Sands Caravan & Camping Gairloch, Wester Ross.

Glengarry Highland Games (16 miles East from Fort William)

- Held in Late-July each year. Tossing the Caber, Highland dancing, Athletics, and Pipe bands.
  https://glengarryhighlandgames.com
  A87, Invergarry.

Halkirk Highland Games (7 miles South of Thurso)

- Held in Late-July each year. Tossing the Caber, Highland dancing, Athletics, and Pipe bands.
  www.halkirkgames.co.uk
  Halkirk Recreation Park, Bridge Street, Halkirk.

Inveraray Highland Games

- Held in Mid-July each year. Tossing the Caber, Highland dancing, Athletics, and Pipe bands.
  http://inveraray-games.co.uk
  Inveraray Castle.

Kenmore Highland Games (7 miles West from Aberfeldy)

- Held in Early-July each year. Tossing the Caber, Highland dancing, Athletics, and Pipe bands.
  http://www.kenmorehighlandgames.com
  Games Park, Kenmore.

Kinlochard Highland Games (24 miles West from Stirling Castle)

- Held in Late-July each year. Tossing the Caber, Highland dancing, Athletics, and Pipe bands.
  www.kinlochard.org
  Kinlochard, Stirling.

Loch Lomond Highland Games

- Held in Early-July each year. Tossing the Caber, Highland dancing, Athletics, and Pipe bands.
  www.llhgb.com
  Moss O Balloch Park, Balloch.

Lochcarron Highland Games

- Held in Late-July each year. Tossing the Caber, Highland dancing, Athletics, and Pipe bands.
  www.lochcarrongames.org.uk
  Attadale Estate, Lochcarron.

Luss (Loch Lomond) Highland Gathering

- Held in Early-July each year. Tossing the Caber, Highland dancing, Athletics, and Pipe bands.
  www.lusshighlandgames.co.uk
  Luss, Loch Lomond.

Markinch Highland Games (20 miles East from Dunfermline Abbey)

- Held in early-June each year. Tossing the Caber, Highland dancing, Athletics, and Pipe bands.
  www.shottshighlandgames.org.uk
  John Dixon Park, Markinch, Glenrothes.

Mull Highland Games

- Held in Mid-July each year. Tossing the Caber, Highland dancing, Athletics, and Pipe bands.
  https://mullhighlandgames.weebly.com
  Erray Park, Tobermory.

Rosneath Peninsula Highland Games
(13 miles West from Helensburgh)

- Held in Mid-July each year. Tossing the Caber, Highland dancing, Athletics, and Pipe bands.
  www.rosneathgames.co.uk
  Rosneath, Helensburgh.

St Andrews Highland Games

- Held in Late-July each year. Tossing the Caber, Highland dancing, Athletics, and Pipe bands.
  www.standrewshighlandgames.co.uk
  Station Park, St Andrews.

South Uist Highland Gathering

- Held in Late-July each year. Tossing the Caber, Highland dancing, Athletics, and Pipe bands.
  www.shottshighlandgames.org.uk
  Askernish Machair, Nr Lochboisdale, South Uist, Outer Hebrides

Stonehaven Highland Games

- All the standard games events including; Highland Dancing, piping competitions, Running Events, Throwing the Hammer, Tossing the Caber and Tug o' War.
  Held each year in late July.
  http://stonehavenhighlandgames.com
  Stonehaven.

Strathconon Highland Games (32 miles from Inverness)

- Held in Late-July each year. Tossing the Caber, Highland dancing, Athletics, and Pipe bands.
  www.strathcononhall.co.uk
  Daybreak Games Field, Strathconon.

Tain Highland Gathering

- Held in Mid-July each year. Tossing the Caber, Highland dancing, Athletics, and Pipe bands.
  www.tainhighlandgathering.com
  Glenmorangie Ground, Tain.

Thornton Highland Gathering(17 miles East from Dunfermline Abbey)

- Held in Early-July each year. Tossing the Caber, Highland dancing, Athletics, and Pipe bands.
  www.shga.co.uk
  Main Street, Thornton.

Tomintoul Highland Games (37 miles South from Elgin)

- Held in Late-July each year. Tossing the Caber, Highland dancing, Athletics, and Pipe bands.
  www.tomintoulhighlandgames.co.uk
  Tomintoul.

August

Aberfeldy Show and Highland Games

- Held in Early-August each year. Tossing the Caber, Highland dancing, Athletics, and Pipe bands.
  www.aberfeldyshowandgames.co.uk
  Wades Park, Aberfeldy.

Aberlour Highland Games

- Held in Early-August each year. Tossing the Caber, Highland dancing, Athletics, and Pipe bands.
  https://aberlourhighlandgames.co.uk
  Aberlour High School, Aberlour.

Aboyne Highland Games (28 miles West of Stonehaven)

- Held in Early-August each year. Tossing the Caber, Highland dancing, Athletics, and Pipe bands.
  www.aboynegames.com
  Village Green, Aboyne.

Argyllshire Highland Games

- Held in Late-August each year. Tossing the Caber, Highland dancing, Athletics, and Pipe bands.
  www.obangames.com
  Mossfield Park, Oban.

Assynt Highland Games (37 miles North from Ullapool)

- Held in Early-August each year. Tossing the Caber, Highland dancing, Athletics, and Pipe bands.
  www.assynthighlandgames.com
  Culag Park, Lochinver.

Ballater Highland Games (38 miles West of Stonehaven)

- Held in Early-August each year. Tossing the Caber, Highland dancing, Athletics, and Pipe bands.
  www.ballaterhighlandgaUnapoolmes.com
  Monaltrie Park, Provost Craig Road, Ballater.

Birnam Highland Games (15 miles North from Perth)

- Held in Late-August each year. Tossing the Caber, Highland dancing, Athletics, and Pipe bands.
  www.birnamhighlandgames.com
  Birnam, Dunkeld.

Bridge of Allan Highland Games (4 miles North from Stirling Castle)

- Held in Early-August each year. Tossing the Caber, Highland dancing, Athletics, and Pipe bands.
  http://bofagames.com
  Strathallan Games Park, Bridge of Allan.

Brodick Highland Games

- Held in Early-August each year. Tossing the Caber, Highland dancing, Athletics, and Pipe bands.
  www.facebook.com/BrodickHighlandGames
  Ormidale Park, Brodick.

Bute Highland Games

- Held in late-August each year. Tossing the Caber, Highland dancing, Athletics, and Pipe bands.
  www.butehighlandgames.org
  The Stadium, High Street, Rothesay.

Castle of Mey Highland Games

- Held in Early-August each year. Tossing the Caber, Highland dancing, Athletics, and Pipe bands.
  www.castleofmey.org.uk
  John O'Groats Showground, The Castle of Mey, Thurso

Cortachy Highland Games (5 miles North from Kirriemuir)

- Held in Mid-August each year. Tossing the Caber, Highland dancing, Athletics, and Pipe bands.
  www.cortachygames.co.uk
  Cortachy Castle Grounds, Kirriemuir.

Crieff Highland Games (18 miles West from Perth)

- Held in Mid-August each year. Tossing the Caber, Highland dancing, Athletics, and Pipe bands.
  www.crieffhighlandgathering.com
  Market Park, Crieff.

Cumnock Highland Games (18 miles West from Ayr)

- Held in Late-August each year. Tossing the Caber, Highland dancing, Athletics, and Pipe bands.
  www.facebook.com/CumnockHighland
  Broomfield Park, Auchinleck Road, Cumnock.

Dornoch Highland Games (43 miles to Inverness)

- Held in Early-August each year. Tossing the Caber, Highland dancing, Athletics, and Pipe bands.
  www.dornochhighlandgames.org
  The Meadows Park, Dornock.

Dundonald Highland Games (Free)
(6 miles West from Kilmarnock)

- Held in late-August each year. Tossing the Caber, Highland dancing, Athletics, and Pipe bands.
  https://dundonald-games.org.uk
  Dundonald Castle, Winehouse Yett, Dundonald.

Dunoon Highland Games

- Held in Late-August each year, this is the largest Highland gathering in the world. Tossing the Caber, Highland dancing, Athletics, and Pipe bands.
  www.cowalgathering.com
  Argyll Road, Kirn, Dunoon.

Glenfinnan Highland Games(17 miles West from Fort William)

- Held in Late-August each year. Tossing the Caber, Highland dancing, Athletics, and Pipe bands.
  www.glenfinnan.org.uk/gathering.asp
  Games Field, Glenfinnan.

Glenisla Highland Games (20 miles North West of Forfar)

- Held in Late-August each year. Tossing the Caber, Highland dancing, Athletics, and Pipe bands.
  www.glenislahighlandgames.co.uk
  The Haugh, Forfar.

Glenurquhart Highland Games (51 miles East from Fort William)

- Held in Late-August each year. Tossing the Caber, Highland dancing, Athletics, and Pipe bands.
  www.glenurquhart-highland-games.co.uk
  Drumnadrochit, Inverness.

Granton on Spey Highland Games (34 miles South from Elgin)

- Held in Late-August each year. Tossing the Caber, Highland dancing, Athletics, and Pipe bands.
  www.visitgrantown.co.uk
  Heithfield Park, Grantown on Spey.

Helmsdale Highland Games (69 Miles to Inverness)

- Held in Mid-August each year. Tossing the Caber, Highland dancing, Athletics, and Pipe bands.
  www.helmsdalegames.co.uk
  Helmsdale.

Inverkeithing Highland Games (14 miles North from the Scott Monument)

- Held in Early-August each year. Tossing the Caber, Highland dancing, Athletics, and Pipe bands.
  http://inverkeithinghighlandgames.com/hg
  Ballast Bank, Inverkeithing.

Isle of Skye Highland Games

- Held in Early-August each year. Tossing the Caber, Highland dancing, Athletics, and Pipe bands.
  www.skye-highland-games.co.uk
  Portree.

Kenmore Highland Games (12 miles North from Aviemore)

- Held in Early-August each year. Tossing the Caber, Highland dancing, Athletics, and Pipe bands.
  https://nethybridge.com/abernethy-highland-games
  Games Field, Nethy Bridge.

Killin Highland Games (45 miles West from Perth)

- Held in Early-August each year. Tossing the Caber, Highland dancing, Athletics, and Pipe bands.
  www.killingames.co.uk
  Breadalbane Park, Killin.

Lonach Highland Gathering & Games (42 miles West from Aberdeen)

- Held on the 4th Saturday of August each year. Tossing the Caber, Highland dancing, Athletics, and Pipe bands.
  www.lonach.org
  Bellabeg Park, Strathdon.

Mallaig & Morar Highland Games (40 miles North/West from Fort William)

- Held in Early-August each year. Tossing the Caber, Highland dancing, Athletics, and Pipe bands.
  www.facebook.com/MallaigAndMorarHighlandGames
  Lovat Field, Morar.

Nairn Highland Games

- Held in Late-August each year. Tossing the Caber, Highland dancing, Athletics, and Pipe bands.
  http://nairnhighlandgames.co.uk
  Nairn Central Links, Nairn.

Newtonmore Highland Games (34 miles North from Blair Atholl)

- Held in Early-August each year. Tossing the Caber, Highland dancing, Athletics, and Pipe bands.
  www.newtonmorehighlandgames.co.uk
  The Eilan, Newtonmore

North Berwick Highland Games(28 miles East from the Scott Monument)

- Held in Early-August each year. Tossing the Caber, Highland dancing, Athletics, and Pipe bands.
  www.northberwickhighlandgames.org
  Recreation Park, Dunbar Road, North Berwick.

Oban Games & Argyllshire Gathering

- Highland games. Held annually on the fourth Thursday in August.
  https://obanlive.com

Perth Highland Games(2 miles North from Perth)

- Held mid-August each year at Scone Palace. Tossing the Caber, Highland dancing, Athletics, Pipe bands and Dancing.
  https://perthhighlandgames.co.uk
  Scone Palace, Perth.

Rannoch Highland Games (21 miles West from Pitlochry)

- Held in Late-August each year. Tossing the Caber, Highland dancing, Athletics, and Pipe bands.
  www.rannochhighlandgathering.co.uk
  Kinloch Rannoch, Pitlochry.

Stirling Highland Games (3 miles East from Stirling Castle)

- Held in Mid-August each year. Tossing the Caber, Highland dancing, Athletics, and Pipe bands.
  www.stirlinghighlandgames.com
  Stirling Games Field, Royal Stuart Way, Stirling.

Strathardle Highland Games (12 miles East from Pitlochry)

- Held in Late-August each year. Tossing the Caber, Highland dancing, Athletics, and Pipe bands.
  https://strathardlehighlandgathering.org.uk
  Bannerfield, Strathardle.

Strathpeffer Highland Games (19 miles to Inverness)

- Held in Early-August each year. Tossing the Caber, Highland dancing, Athletics, and Pipe bands.
  www.strathpefferhighlandgathering.com
  Castle Leod, Strathpeffer.

World Pipe Band Competition (1-mile from George Square)

- World Pipe Band Competition held each year in August and hosting pipe bands from all over the World.
  www.theworlds.co.uk
  Greendyke Street, Saltmarket.

September

Blairgowrie & Rattray Highland Games (16 miles North from Perth)

- Held in Early-September each year. Tossing the Caber, Highland dancing, Athletics, and Pipe bands.
  www.blairgowriehighlandgames.co.uk
  Bogles Field, Essendy Road, Blairgowrie.

Braemar Gathering

- Annual Highland games held in Braemar on the first Saturday in September and traditionally attended by the British Royal Family.
  www.braemargathering.org
  Princess Royal and Duke of Fife Memorial Park, Braemar.

Invercharron Highland Games (39 Miles to Inverness)

- Held in Late-September each year. Tossing the Caber, Highland dancing, Athletics, and Pipe bands.
  www.invercharronhighlandgames.co.uk
  Bonar Bridge.

Peebles Highland Games (23 miles South from the Scott Monument)

- Held in Early-September each year. Tossing the Caber, Highland dancing, Athletics, and Pipe bands.
  www.peebleshighlandgames.com
  Hay Lodge Park, Old Town, Peebles.

Pitlochry Highland Games

- Held in Mid-September each year. Tossing the Caber, Highland dancing, Athletics, and Pipe bands.
  www.pitlochryhighlandgames.co.uk
  Ferry Road, Pitlochry.

Chapter 12

Festivals and Celebrations

Listed by month, so you can find them or avoid them, your choice.

January

Burns Night

- Held all over Scotland and indeed all over the world to celebrate the birthday (25 January 1759) of the Scots poet Robert Burns. With poetry readings, haggis, kilts and whisky. www.scotland.org

Celtic Connections

- This is the largest winter festival of its kind. Each year there are over 300 events around the city, including ceilidhs (traditional Scottish dance event), talks, art shows, workshops and concerts. Heldmid-January to early February each year. www.celticconnections.com

Up Helly Aa

- A series of fire festivals held throughout the island from January to March each year, with the main one held on the last Tuesday of January in Lerwick.
www.uphellyaa.org

February

Glasgow Film Festival

- From new blockbusters to avant-garde arthouse, live talks and rare cult classics. Held from late February to early March.
https://glasgowfilm.org

March

Aberdeen Jazz Festival

- Showcasing live jazz performances with musicians from around the world, held at several different venues. Held in March each year.
www.aberdeenjazzfestival.com
Various venues, Aberdeen.

Fife Whisky Festival(31 miles East from Dunfermline Abbey)

- Held in Early-March each year. This is a 3-day Festival for the appreciation of Whisky. https://fifewhiskyfestival.com
  St Catherine Street, Cupar.

April

Shetland Folk Festival

- Various venues throughout Shetland. Held late April, early May each year. www.shetlandfolkfestival.com

Spirit of Speyside Whisky Festival

- Various locations throughout Moray Speysideincluding many famous distilleries. Held late April, early May each year. www.spiritofspeyside.com

May

Aberdeen May Festival

- Featuring films, food, Gaelic, literature, music, science and sport. Held in late May each year. www.abdn.ac.uk/mayfestival
  Various venues, Aberdeen.

Campbeltown Malts Festival

- Held annually every May. A 3-day celebration of Glengyle, Glen Scotia and Springbank. Campbeltown's 3 whisky distilleries. www.explorecampbeltown.com

Edinburgh Whisky Stramash

- Held annually in Late-May. Set in the opulent and historic Surgeon's Hall on Nicholson Street. www.thewhiskystramash.com

Feis Ile

- Islay Festival with; Ceilidhs, Gaelic lessons, Golf, Music, Poetry and Whisky. Held annually in late May. www.islayfestival.com

Hebridean Whisky Trail Festival

- Held in Late-May each year. With 4 distilleries situated on different Hebridean islands. https://hebrideanwhisky.com

Highland Whisky Festival

- Eight-day festival held in Mid-May each year. With8 distilleries situated on the North Coast 500 each hosting a different day of the festival. www.highlandwhiskyfestival.co.uk

Orkney Folk Festival

- With local Orcadian and international artists this 4-day festival is held late-May each year. www.orkneyfolkfestival.com

June

Edinburgh International Film Festival

- This two weeks-long festival is the oldest continuously running Film Festival in the world. Held annually in late-June. www.edfilmfest.org.uk

Edinburgh Whisky Festival

- Held annually in Early-June. Held in the Assembly rooms on George Street. https://thewhiskylounge.com

Royal Highland Show (8 miles West of the Scott Monument, Edinburgh)

- Scotland's largest agricultural show held at Ingliston show grounds, attracting over 1,000 exhibitors, 4,500 head of livestock, and up to 200,000 visitors each year. www.royalhighlandshow.org

Scottish Traditional Boat Festival (43 West of Inverness)

- With boats (competitive sailing), music, crafts, food and drinkheld annually in late-June in Portsoy. www.stbfportsoy.org

Selkirk Common Riding

- Held annually in early-June and dating back over 400 years to the time of the "Burleymen", Burgh Law men who had the task of ensuring no one was encroaching on the town's common lands. Also remembered is the return of only one man from the battle of Flodden in 1513 after 80 men from Selkirk followed James IV into battle. That one man (Fletcher) returned, weary and wounded but bearing a captured English flag which he raised aloft and then cast to the ground. The Riding of the Marches lasts about 4½ hours and the riders return to the Market Place. Celebrations continue into the next day with horse racing, and professional games. https://returntotheridings.co.uk/selkirk-common-riding

St Magnus Festival

- Orkney's celebration of the arts held annually in mid-June, with venues all over Orkney. www.stmagnusfestival.com

July

Cantilena Festival

- Chamber Music performed by Cantilena's professional musicians and students of the Royal Conservatoire of Scotland. Held annually in July at various venues on Islay. www.cantilenafestival.co.uk

HebCelt Festival

- Four-day Traditional Celtic Music Festival usually held in July at various venues on the Hebrides. www.hebceltfest.com

Stonehaven Folk Festival

- Over 50 events from on stage performances to informal performances in pubs and around the harbor. Held each year in mid-July. www.stonehavenfolkfestival.co.uk *Stonehaven.*

Tarbert Seafood Festival

- Held Annually in the first full weekend of July. www.tarbertlochfyne.com

August

If you don't like crowds, then avoid Edinburgh in August.

Edinburgh International Book Festival

- With over 100 free events held around the city over the last two weeks of August. www.edbookfest.co.uk

Edinburgh Fringe Festival

The Edinburgh Festival Fringe is the world's largest arts festival, held over the last three weeks of August and featuring more than 50,000 performances of 3,500 different shows at over 300 venues throughout the city. www.eif.co.uk

Edinburgh International Festival

- The Festival's program features the finest performers and ensembles from the worlds of dance, opera, music and theatre. Held annually in the last three weeks of August. www.eif.co.uk

Largs Viking Festival

- Held annually in the last week of August and the first week of September in the town of Largs. To commemorate the Battle of Largs, the last ever Viking invasion on British soil. https://largsvikingfestival.org

Mull of Kintyre Music Festival

- Held annually every August in Campbeltown. www.explorecampbeltown.com

The Royal Military Tattoo

- Held annually every August and performed by British, Commonwealth and international Military bands in Edinburgh Castle. www.edintattoo.co.uk

September

Islay Jazz Festival

- Held annually in September at various venues on Islay. www.islayjazzfestival.co.uk

Spirit of Speyside Whisky Festival

- Various locations throughout Moray Speysideincluding many famous distilleries. Held late April, early May each year. www.spiritofspeyside.com

Spirit of Speyside Distilled: Food & Drink

- Various locations throughout Moray Speyside. Held Early September each year. www.spiritofspeyside.com

Spirit of the North Festival

- Various locations throughout Moray Speyside. Held Late-September each year. www.spiritofspeyside.com

Tarbert Music Festival

- Featuring contemporary and traditional Scottish Music. Held Annually in mid-September. www.tarbertlochfyne.com

October

Royal National Mòd

- The Mòd is a celebration of [Scottish] Gaelic language and culture, with a different host city/town each year. www.ancomunn.co.uk

Scottish International Storytelling Festival

- Twelve-day celebration held at the end of October each year with storytelling, oral traditions. Bringing together Scottish and International storytellers and musicians. www.sisf.org.uk

December

Hogmanay Street Party, Edinburgh

- This is the big one, with hundreds of thousands of people gathered to welcome in the New Year. The party starts at 7:30pm on Hogmanay (New Year's Eve) and carries on into the wee hours of January 1st. Be entertained by international bands, DJs and street performers. At midnight a spectacular fireworks display illuminates the sky over Edinburgh Castle.
www.edinburghshogmanay.com
Princes Street Gardens.

Some other Hogmanay Parties to consider

- The whole of Scotland celebrates the turning of the year over a 3-day period with huge parties or just dropping in on the neighbors. Most of the cities or towns will have something going on, here are a few of the larger towns that hold a celebration; Aberdeen, Falkirk, Lerwick, Musselburgh, Stirling, Stonehaven, Stromness.
www.scotland.org/events/hogmanay/hogmanay-events

Stonehaven Fire Festival

- The town has a very different way of welcoming in the new year. As the bells ring in the new year at midnight on December 31st around 40 men and women parade up and down the main street swinging flaming fireballs around their heads.
  http://stonehavenfireballs.co.uk
  Stonehaven.

Chapter 13

Additional Information

Driving an electric car?

I have mentioned which towns/cities have charging stations, but for a more comprehensive list/map see the following website.
https://chargeplacescotland.org/live-map

Midges

As you would expect from the country that brought you "Nessie" the loch Ness monster, the Highland midge" has taken on an almost mythical status. I have heard it described as being about the size of a period (full stop) at the end of a sentence, with the teeth of an alligator. First things first, midges do not transmit diseases to humans, about the only thing transmitted will be the tall tales that you'll tell when you return home. The "midgie" as it is known in Scotland is so small that if you are walking, the wind of your passing will stop it from landing on you. If there is a slight breeze you are safe, in fact about the only time that you are likely to get bitten is while asleep (mainly if you are camping). Almost every hotel in the highlands of Scotland will have a warning about keeping your windows closed, because of the midges.

After all that, the bite doesn't hurt it just itches. You can use any insect repellant that would work for mosquitoes to keep them at bay or the old traditional method is to crush bog myrtle leaves in your palms and rub it on the exposed areas of skin. Which I have done to good effect in the past.
Growing up in Scotland and travelling back there on many trips, the midges was pretty much a non-event, until the summer of 2016. We stopped at Kinloch Lodge on the Isle of Skye for the night, and I noticed midges (lots of them) coming in through the windows, they were so small the seals couldn't stop them. I went to the local village to a grocery store for repellant, but they had none (obviously the locals are tougher than me). On the way back to the hotel I saw Bog Myrtle growing and stopped to pick some.
Back in the room I crushed some leaves on a few small branches, which I intertwined on the portable fan and pointed it at our bed, we were not bitten that night.
Our friend David was in another part of the hotel, so I called him and told him what to do, he declined. He got badly bitten that night.
The next night was spent at the Inverbeg Hotel in the village of Luss on Loch Lomond, that night we had no problems. The following morning when we were trying to get our bags into the car, we were attacked by more midges, than I have ever seen. They may be small, but us three adults jumped in the car and drove away as fast as we could. Un-fortunately they had come with us and we had to drive along with the windows open to try and get rid of them.
Next time we go to Scotland I am taking some mosquito repellant, better safe than sorry.
They are not a problem during the winter in Scotland as the first frost usually kills them off.

Nationwide bus companies

- Citylink
  www.citylink.co.uk

- Megabus
  https://uk.megabus.com

- National
  www.nationalexpress.com

- Stagecoach
  www.stagecoachbus.com

ScotRail

- National Rail Enquiries
  www.scotrail.co.uk

Passports

Take a photo of your passport with your phone that way if you lose your Passport, you have your Passport information on your phone.
If you are worried about keeping that on your phone you could e-mail it (and your itinerary) to someone you trust back home. That way if you lose your passport, they will have the information available to help you get back home.

Bibliography

I have put links to all the places listed in this book and would like to thank them all for the information I have gathered in here. The information in this book is a snapshot of each of the places listed and for more in depth information, I suggest you go to the website of the place that you are interested in.
I would also like to thank the following sources;

Affric Kintail Way
www.affrickintailway.com

Along Dusty Roads
www.alongdustyroads.com

Annandale Way
http://annandaleway.org

Arran Coastal Way
www.coastalway.co.uk

Atlas Obscura
www.atlasobscura.com

Ayrshire Coastal Path
http://ayrshirecoastalpath.org

Berwickshire Coastal Path
https://walkscottishborders.com/route/berwickshire-coastal-path

Borders Abbeys Trail
www.bordersabbeysway.com

Canmore
https://canmore.org.uk

Cape Wrath Trail
https://capewrathtrailguide.org

Cateran Trail
www.walkthecaterantrail.com

Celtic Castles
www.celticcastles.com

ChargePlace Scotland
https://chargeplacescotland.org

CityLink Buses
www.citylink.co.uk

Cowal way
www.cowalway.co.uk

Dumfries and Galloway Council
www.dumgal.gov.uk

ebooks Visit Scotland
https://ebooks.visitscotland.com

East Highland Way
www.easthighlandway.com

Encyclopedia Britannica
www.britannica.com

Fife Coastal Path
www.fifecoastalpath.co.uk

Filmed in Edinburgh
www.filmedinburgh.org

Find a Grave
www.findagrave.com

Glasgow Life
www.glasgowlife.org.uk

Historic Environment Scotland
www.historicenvironment.scot

Historic UK
www.historic-uk.com

John Muir way
http://johnmuirway.org

Kintyre Way
www.kintyreway.com

Live Borders
www.liveborders.org.uk

Loch Lomond Seaplanes
www.lochlomondseaplanes.com

Long Distance Walking Association
www.ldwa.org.uk

Megabus Buses
https://uk.megabus.com

Moray Coast Trail
www.morayways.org.uk/moray-coast-trail.asp

National Buses
www.nationalexpress.com

National Trust Scotland
www.nts.org.uk

Orkney.com
www.orkney.com

People Make Glasgow
https://peoplemakeglasgow.com

Rob Roy Way
www.robroyway.com

Scotrail
www.scotrail.co.uk

Shetland Amenity Trust
www.shetlandamenity.org

Southern Upland Way
www.southernuplandway.gov.uk

Speyside Way
www.speysideway.org

St Cuthbert's Way
www.stcuthbertsway.info

Stagecoach Buses
www.stagecoachbus.com

The Great Glen Way
www.highland.gov.uk/ggw

The North Coast 500
www.northcoast500.com

The West Highland Way
www.westhighlandway.org

Trip Advisor
www.tripadvisor.com

The Trossachs
https://trossachs.co.uk

Virtual Hebrides
www.virtualheb.co.uk

Visit Britain
www.visitbritain.com

Visit Outer Hebrides
www.visitouterhebrides.co.uk

Visit Scotland
www.visitscotland.com

Walk Highlands
www.walkhighlands.co.uk

Watch me See
https://watchmesee.com

Wikivoyage
https://en.wikivoyage.org

Wikipedia
www.wikipedia.org

Biography

Paul Bissett was born in Edinburgh, Scotland and raised in the village of Blackness on the river Forth. At the age of seventeen he embarked upon a twenty-three-year career in the British Royal Navy, which took him all over the world. He has lived and worked in seven different countries.
He has, at various times been; a mountain guide; made and installed kilns in Australia; an instructor in Saudi Arabia; a Documentation Manager for a software company in Taiwan; and in the USA been a salesman for Sears, a firefighter, an Emergency Medical Technician (EMT), a jewelry store manager, senior case manager for the National Expert Witness Network based in Paradise, California and recently became an Independent Contractor for International Network in Advance-Gaming Inc., covering California.
Outside of work, he conducts Celtic and Scottish weddings. Hosts whiskey tastings, in California, Nevada and Oregon. For fun, he researches whisky bars, writes/edits a whisky newsletter that go out to readers in ten different countries. He also gives talks on all things Scottish and has been the Master of Ceremonies at many events all over the world, including the Las Vegas Celtic Games (twice).
He currently lives in Yuba City, California, with his wife Tracey and their three dogs, Heather, Hamish and Luna.

Also, by Paul Bissett;

A Whisky Might Not Fix Things, But It's Worth A Shot! - Whisk(e)y related: Anecdotes, Humor, Jokes, Memes, Quotes, Toasts & Trivia.

Cigar Traveler - A guide to Cigar lounges in USA.

From Milngavie to Midges - Hiking the "West Highland Way."

Hiking with Nessie - Hiking the "Great Glen Way."

Scotland's Single Malt Whisky Distilleries – A guide.

Whisky Timeline - Whisk(e)y distilleries around the world and when they were founded.

Whisky Traveler - A guide to Whisk(e)y bars around the world.

Winter's Bite - A children's novel. A modern-day adventure set in Scotland and based on Scottish mythology.

All are available at www.amazon.com

My email is; paulwbissett@outlook.com

My website is; www.scot-talks.com

Printed in Poland
by Amazon Fulfillment
Poland Sp. z o.o., Wrocław

61895002R00291